How To Be A Responsibly Powerful Bitch

Take Your Life to New Heights

aka

Check Yourself Before You Wreck Yourself

Dr. Troy Byer

How To Be A Responsibly Powerful Bitch
& Take Your Life to New Heights

Cover By: Sign. Yra Design
Edited By: Lauren Krom & Frank Match
Book Layout By: Sunil Kumar

ISBN-13: 978-0980176391
ISBN-10: 0980176395

I dedicate this book to
my wonderful ex-mother-in-law
Dorothy Burg
who has been a beacon of unwavering
Love, Light & Guidance in my life
&
In Memory of
my grandmothers Elizabeth Messenger
& Corinth Hampton

CONTENTS

CHAPTER 1
THE RECKLESS BITCH SNAG

You Always Get What You Settle For

> "Emotions consist of patterns of physiological changes and accompanying behaviors – or at least urges to perform these behaviors."
>
> - Carlson & Birknett, 2017, p. 345

According to recent research done by psychologists and neuroscientists from Glasgow University, there are actually four basic human emotions and not six as originally recorded (Jack, 2014). Omitting the emotions of disgust and surprise from the previous list, the newly confirmed four basic human emotions are anger, sadness, happiness and fear. Unlike happiness and fear, emotions such as sadness and anger in women can be physiologically triggered by hormonal imbalances. What that means for us women is, regardless of our commitment to being angelic, halo-wearing, mothers, wives and daughters, when our menstrual or menopausal cycles impact our hormonal balances - we have the instantaneous potential of transforming into weeping willows or Satan's out-of-control angry sister. Unlike anger, sadness poses little to no threat when it comes to our personal safety. No matter how you slice it, anger can almost always lead to danger and when our hormone-influenced anger is coupled with upsetting external factors, "hell hath no fury!"

This book has everything to do with teaching women how to

keep their anger in check be it hormone imbalance influenced anger or the result of upsetting external factors – or both. To be crystal clear, in check anger can be a good thing. Anger out of check, not so good. I am living proof that out of check anger is an extremely reckless emotion that can take us places we literally have prayed we would never go. In May 2006, I found myself in handcuffs on my way to jail. I was arrested for fighting with my boyfriend; let's just call him, Ron. Ron was my son's "manny" - male Nanny - and I fell in deep "like" with him, mostly for the wrong reasons. I loved the way he loved my son and I loved how he believed in my professional aspirations. Truth be told, I was also a very lonely, single, lost, 42-year-old woman who secretly felt like a huge failure. Right. Okay. Wrong. Wrong. Wrong and wrong again.

At the time, I had just moved into the 2.6 million dollar home that my ex-husband had purchased for our son and me. The nearly five-thousand-square-foot home was far too large for just the two of us, but it was the house I insisted on having because it looked like a queen's castle. I loved everything about it, or so I thought. Because I did not take my ex-husband to the cleaners during our divorce, he promised me that when and if his career turned out as he hoped it would, he would buy me the house of my dreams. He kept his word.

Ron was pretty much always at the house chilling with my son and me. We felt like a family, and I knew Ron had a thing for me. I thought he was cute, but he was also seventeen years younger than me. His age, combined with the fact that he was my son's Manny, made it all the harder for me to give into his subtle but sexy as hell advances. Finally, the day came when his fraternity-like roommate situation went awry, and I suggested he move in with us. It just felt like the right thing to do, and at that point, I was like, "screw all the wrong reasons."

Several hours before my arrest, Ron and I stood hand-in-hand as he blew out the twenty-four candles on his Sweet Lady Jane birthday cake I custom ordered for him. I was beyond proud of the party that I hosted for Ron, a party that covertly seconded as our coupling coming-out party to my community of suspicious minds. From all the joy and love present that day, no one could have ever predicted my waking up in a jail cell the next morning. In retrospect, the experience brings life to Adele's lyrics, "only yesterday was the time of our lives." In a matter of out-of-control anger inflicted minutes, it was all over.

When You Call the Po-Po, Someone's Gotta Go-Go

Shortly after the last party guest left, Ron and I got into a heated argument. Realizing he was drunk, I asked him to behave or spend the night with one of his guy friends at their place. Also slightly under the influence, my tolerance for bullshit from a boy I just introduced as my man and hosted an expensive birthday party for was very low. Sparing you the details, I will jump right to the juicy part at which I decided that Ron really had to go. He refused my demand and continued to be belligerent. Sensing the onset of a huge fight, I called the cops. Let me just pause here to say, in the ghetto environment that I come from, when a female calls the cops, without a doubt the male is forced to leave or taken to jail.

I was certain my calling the cops would be enough to scare Ron out the door. No such luck. To the contrary, my calling the cops angered him and the fight I had anticipated was seconds away from being full-blown. As soon as I disconnected the call, Ron grabbed me and threw me on the couch. He pinned me down, holding my hands above my head. "Calm down!" he screamed over and over again. I don't know about you, but three of the worst things anyone – especially a dude - can say to me when I am upset are, "you're being way too sensitive", "you're just like your mother," or "calm down!"

For a minute or three, I had no problem with Ron holding me down on the couch. I knew he would eventually have to let me go because the cops were on their way anyway. However, after what must have been the twentieth time his drunk ass spit the words, "calm down!" in my face, I screamed back, "stop fucking telling me to calm down in my own house!" He shoved his knee into my throat, choking me. I began to gasp for air. He then, seething, reminded me that my beautiful dream house was not really my house because I could never afford a house like that on my own. His words sent me into a fit of rage, "Aw shit, it's on now!" I said through gritted teeth. Ron soon learned he had just opened a whole can of whup ass! Thankful for my martial arts training, I knew exactly how to free myself from his grip. Biting his forearm forced him to loosen his grip on my left hand. I then proceeded to beat his ass like a woman possessed. When I heard the cops pull up, I remembered thinking, "my heroes are here." I ran to the door, greeting the officers with uncontrollable sobs and demanding, "he's in there, please just get him out of here!" Know The Law Before You Lean On The Law.

Well, getting him out of there was not how it went down at all. I was not aware that there was a new law mandating that whenever the police arrive at a home due to a domestic violence dispute, one of the two people involved in the altercation has to be arrested if there are visible signs of injury. The person arrested is the person who the police decide is the primary aggressor. Because Ron had more wounds on his body than I had on mine, it was assumed that I was the primary aggressor, which meant that I was the one who was going to jail. Needless to say, trying to explain that I was only acting out of self-defense fell on deaf ears. The officer's only response was, "save your story for the judge."

I think it's worth mentioning that I am no stranger to arrests or the prison system. I have two brothers on my mother's side who have been arrested and incarcerated more times than I care to count. At the age of twelve when I was finally taken away from my mother for child abuse, I went to live with my estranged father, who was a police officer at the time. I quickly became a volunteer Police Explorer so I could ride patrol with my dad, who arrested people all the time. I remember feeling so sorry for my brothers and other people I often witnessed being cuffed and caged like animals behind bars. I used to pray that such a humiliating experience would never happen to me - and yet, there I was.

As I sat in the back of the patrol car, cuffed and en route to the station, I was in total shock and disbelief. Ron's recently homeless ass was left in my dream home, sleeping in my dream bed, and I was on my way to jail. If I could have held my breath long enough to suffocate and die in the back seat of that patrol car, I would have indeed. On the lighter side of things, I think it is worth mentioning, the woman in charge of my booking process at the prescient recognized me from my starring role on the former hit ABC television series, Dynasty. She had been a big fan of my work and even asked me for an autograph. She also informed me that she would insist that I be placed in the VIP jail cell, fearing for my safety in common population. Then, she told me my timing for the VIP cell was perfect because Paris Hilton had just recently checked out after completing her "cute little sentence."

That night, as I lay my head on the pillow presumably used by Paris Hilton, I had so many thoughts running through my mind at once, it seemed as if the room was spinning. I found myself wondering why the jail cell did not have a mirror. I wondered why I allowed others to upset me so easily. I tried to imagine what the steel toilet would feel like if I sat on it. I began to wonder why, once I was upset, I allowed my anger to escalate to the point of no return. In my heart, I knew this was hardly the first time that I had allowed my anger to get out of control. It had happened far too many times before, and to my embarrassment and shame, it was starting to happen even more so lately. People had told me in the past that I was an angry person, and with every ounce of cuteness I could muster; I would reply, "clearly, you don't know me. I'm the sweetest person I know." However, that night in that tiny cement block cell, I had to finally tell myself the truth. I had to admit that after years and years of practice, I was an angry, out-of-control, reckless bitch. I now understand; I never wanted to admit that I had a problem because, at the time, I had no idea that I could organically do something about it.

My Anger Justifications

I had been participating in transformational work for decades. I was even leading programs from time-to-time for a major global organization. I was great at transforming the lives of others, but when it came to my life and my issues, there was always something missing, and I couldn't quite figure out what it was. After finally admitting I had a problem, I remember sitting up, leaning against the cement wall, and talking out loud. I suddenly became obsessed with the "why" of it all. "Why was I so fucking angry?" I softly asked myself. In an instant, I saw myself riding around on that tricycle I used to ride when I was a four-year-old kid actor on the PBS hit series, Sesame Street. "That's it!" I thought, "I'm pissed off because instead of going to school like normal kids and seeing my friends, my mom forced me to go to work on Sesame Street so I could make money to pay her bills and buy her drugs." I could feel my heart beat faster as I remembered the stupid things I had to do on that show, like the time Kermit the Frog tried to get me to admit that 1 + 1 = 3. He used every trick in the book to convince me to change my mind. I insisted that 1 + 1 would forever be 2. He finally agreed that I was right. The director yelled, "cut!" Next thing I know, Jim Henson, the creator of The Muppets and the voice of Kermit at that time, dropped Kermit on his face and gave me a big high five saying, "nobody's going to fool Troy." All present applauded, but I nearly burst into tears. I felt so sad for myself. I could not understand for the life of me why anyone would want to make me look like a fool on national television.

I wish I could say that was my first and only incident like that on Sesame Street, but it wasn't. There was the time Bob wanted me to pretend I did not know how to tie my shoes so that we could teach the little boys and girls at home watching while he taught me. What Bob didn't know was that every time I pretended I did not know something on the show, after that episode would air, kids would tease me at school and call me names like, Stupid and Dummy. I guess it is safe to say that, in many ways, Sesame Street significantly contributed to my anger and becoming a reckless bitch.

Looking back at my childhood a bit more, I realized that I was angry at my father for abandoning me at the age of two. I was angry with my mother for allowing her men to molest me for months at a time from age six to nine, and then accusing me of being a liar when I told her what was happening. I was also angry with my mother for trying to marry me off at the age of eleven to a 42-year-old man who lived in a foreign country in exchange for a washer and dryer. It was becoming clear to me that I had some serious mother issues. I then realized I was angry with my mother for all the years she beat me until I bled, and the time she beat me so badly with a chair that she broke my leg. Enough mom stuff. I then switched back to my dad and realized that I was angry with my estranged father for taking me out of foster care and assuming full custody of me only to be far more neglectful and just as abusive as my mother.

On a roll with nowhere to go, I figured, "why stop now?" I finally admitted I was angry with all the people I looked up to who told me I would never be smart enough to be a doctor or lawyer, as I had longed to be. They urged me to try and get back into acting or learn to type so I could be a good secretary. I refused to be a secretary, so I was angry that I had no choice but to return to show business after high school. I failed miserably as an actress, writer, and director in a profession I didn't even want to be a part of. And now, drum roll, please....! For the first time, I admitted that I was also angry that my first true love, the legendary artist and my on-again, off-again boyfriend of five years, Prince, broke up with me on screen. I thought we were just exchanging dialogue and acting out a scene for one of his extended music videos as we had so often done before. The next thing I know, he married Mayte, the young girl who I thought we simply regarded and adored as our little sister. Yes, I was really pissed off about that. I also came to terms with the fact that I was angry because, when I finally got over Prince and was able to love again, my marriage ended in divorce just five years later.

The Think Tank

I had no idea I was angry about so many things. I mean, who sets aside time to think about all the things they are angry about? Jail cells are great structures for thinking because there is absolutely nothing else to do besides, as I mentioned, wonder where the mirror went and what the cold metal toilet might feel like on my bare bum.

I still think it is so perfectly divine that one of the most powerful self-reflective sessions of my life took place in a mirrorless jail cell.

After exploring the reasons for my anger, I began to think about my present and my future. What a surprise, just thinking about my present and my future was making me angry. Okay, here we go. I switched sitting positions on the cardboard mattress and relentlessly pushed up against the internal discomfort that was once again elevating my heart rate. "Well, this is news!" I said out loud as tears stung my eyes. I forced myself to admit that I had settled for Ron because I did not believe I was worthy of anyone better. Ouch. That was a punch in the gut. My gut-wrenching sobs confirmed, yep, that's exactly what that was. Another truth - I had no idea how truly uncomfortable and angry it made me knowing that the multi-million dollar house I called home was the byproduct of promising not to destroy my son's father during our divorce. What a shitty context that was to build a dream on. Deducing it even further, I realized my dream house would always serve as a structural reminder of my failed marriage. Ugh! No matter how I sliced it, how I got that house totally sucked. And finally, the real fur-ball-of-it-all was that I did not want to admit that I was angry because I had no idea what I was going to do with the rest of my life. I felt like an absolute, one hundred percent failure living in a castle I could not afford, and as a result I felt like a f-r-a-u-d. Ouch. Ouch. Ouch.

When Things Fall Apart, Let Them

My jail stay was a quick and unforgettable fourteen hours. A week later, I stood before the expressionless judge and listened as he sentenced me to a 52-week anger management program. My first instinct was to firmly state, "Your Honor Judge Sir, I do not have an anger problem." Remembering my new truth, I smiled instead. He closed my paper-thin file and dismissed me with the slightest tap of his gavel. Keeping it real, admitting I had a problem was a great first step, but in no way cured me of my problem. During the first few weeks of the program, I was miserable. I was still angry I got arrested, and I was even angrier that I had to attend the stupid meetings. Every week I would walk through the door and plop my limp angry body on the couch with my eyes glued to the clock. I could not wait to get out of that place and away from the women who reminded me way too much of myself and my sadness and pain. Thankfully, Ron and I were not together, and he had long since moved out because there were many times when I left those anger management meetings angry as hell and eager to take it out on him. Clearly, the program was not working on me - or so I thought.

Halfway through the program, I had what Carl Jung refers to as the "dark night of the soul." It was my forty-second birthday, and I had a meltdown. Note, I did not have an out-of-control anger episode; I had a gut-wrenching melt down. In retrospect, I now understand, the anger fits I had been having were subconscious attempts to avoid confronting the profound sadness I had suppressed for the last forty plus years. On that night, I let it all out. I threw myself on the ground, and I cried and cried and cried, and then I cried some more. I felt deep sadness for all those things that I really just thought I was angry about: from the abuse I suffered at the hands of my mother, to the disappointment I experienced when I finally met my father, to Prince dumping me during an acting scene on camera, to my divorce, and so on. The sadness was so unbearably heavy. I felt as if I simply could not go on with my life.

My sister and my personal assistant came by to take me out for my birthday dinner that night. They were astounded to see me sprawled out on the floor, sobbing uncontrollably. They wanted to hug me and make everything okay. I wanted them to leave. It finally took me being mean and angry to send them away. I knew what I needed. I needed to cry in solitude from my soul, for my soul, to my soul. It was a cry I had never experienced before, and as much as it hurt, it felt so damn good to just let it all out and to let all that sadness go. I did not know it at the time, but I was actually experiencing spiritual labor pains. Something beautiful was trying to be born.

Several hours later, after I finished crying for myself and all the things I thought I was angry about, I was surprised to find myself crying for the women in the court-mandated anger management program. I cried because 99% of the women in the program were not outlaws with previous criminal records. Some of them were doctors, lawyers, nurses, housewives, teachers - all simply normal women like me. Normal women with abnormally painful past experiences left unresolved. Experiences that still hurt and were in desperate need of being unconcealed, revealed and healed.

As I continued to cry for these women that I loved as if they were truly me, I felt the sadness their anger was masking. I felt the shame and embarrassment their anger had caused them. I felt their hopelessness, and then, once again, realized my own. Feeling hopeless, I sobbed out loud, "I wish I could help them!" And then I heard this voice say, "Troy, get up! Get up right now, or you better plan on forever staying down!" I paused. I looked around. "WTH?" I whispered harshly. The voice continued, "Look Bitch, right here, right now, you decide! In this moment, you must decide who you want to be and what you want to do. You are either going to continue to be reckless, or you are going to stop the bullshit and get powerfully responsible for your life. It's now or never, girlfriend. Call it! What do you want!?" Without hesitation, I crawled to my knees, tears and snot flying everywhere, and from the bottom of my heart I remembered screaming, "I want to make a difference for all the women who hurt like me. That's what I want! I want to help stop the hurt!" The voice replied, "Then get up and fucking do it!"

The Birth, The Growth

That night, I believe I gave birth to a purpose that is so beautiful that to this day, it still takes my breath away. From that night on, pursuing my purpose with unbridled passion has been the air that I breathe. I now understand everything that ever happened to me happened for me! I needed to experience various forms of abuse, anger, abandonment, sadness, all of it because today my greatest strength as a teacher does not come from the ten years of intense academic training that has led to my currently being a doctoral candidate in clinical psychology. My greatest strength and power as a teacher comes from my on-the-court life experiences and the level of unwavering empathy I get to bring to my interactions with the thousands of angry women I now work with around the world.

As I write this, I am moved to tears by the privilege it is also to share with you that I now teach the very court-mandated anger management program the judge sentenced me to eleven years ago. Every week I have the privilege of introducing myself to new court-mandated participants as they walk through the door and plop their limp angry bodies on the couch with their eyes glued to the clock. There is no sweeter moment than when I get to inform these women that I once sat in the very seats they are now sitting in and witness their instant shift in demeanor. Knowing that I know them, that I am them, and that I am truly on their team is the difference they need. The difference they need to trust again, to heal, to lean courageously into their "dark night of the soul," to be born again. Once in a while, someone will snarl and ask, "Why the hell would you ever come back here?" My response is simple. "I come back here so you, and other women who have never been here, will never have to."

We Know Who We Are

I wrote this book for the same reasons that I teach the class. If any of what you have read so far does not feel familiar to you, then this book can be your sure fire way to make sure it never does. If anything you have read so far resonates with you, then for sure, this book is for you. I dedicate this book to every woman who has ever allowed her anger to get her into a situation that her out-of-control ass could not get her out of. Surely, you remember that time, or better yet those times, when you overreacted and said that thing or did that thing that destroyed your game. Yes, I'm talking about that monkey wrench that shut your shit down because your sassy ass refused to pipe down. As a result of your inability to put yourself in check, once again you return to your corner a hot mess drenched with a false sense of righteousness trying to silence that inner voice of yours as it loudly whispers, "You are such a reckless bitch! WTF is wrong with you?!" It actually continues and continues. "How are you ever going to have the life you want if you keep pushing people away with your reckless bitch ways?" Your answer: "It was (him, her, it, them) not me. If they can't handle my truth or my personality, I don't need them. I'd rather be alone." Lie. Lie. Lie. Lie. If you tell yourself even half of the truth, you will admit that alienating people rarely feels good and is awfully hard to justify, especially if managing your reckless ass would have almost certainly produced a far better result.

Throughout this book, I want to focus on four things. It is my commitment to you, the reader, to fully develop and expand upon the following ideas:

1. To address the reasons why we, as women, do not chill out when we know darn well we are seconds away from irreversible damage or danger.

2. To demonstrate exactly how formerly reckless bitches can have the lives they want by upgrading their bitch status

from reckless bitch to Responsibly Powerful Bitch.

3. To help you understand the origin of your anger triggers and buttons and identify them before they emotionally and blindly take you hostage.
4. To teach you how to access your anger as a powerful source for creating a life you absolutely love

CHAPTER 2
UNDERSTANDING THE BITCH

Bitch-Scription

Just to be clear, we all have the potential to be reckless bitches and Responsible Bitches. As far as I am concerned, the reckless bitch and the Responsible Bitch exist on the same hand, just different sides. Visually speaking, the reckless bitch is the side of the hand that will backhand you. The Responsible Bitch is the open hand, palm up, offering to help you. Now would also be a good time for me to let you know, I do not believe we, as women, are bitches twenty-four seven, three hundred and sixty-five days out of the year. I am certain, however, that being a bitch is very much like being a driver of a car. You are not always the driver, but when you are driving, you always have two options when presented with challenges, stressors or threats. You can be a reckless driver, or you can be a responsible driver. The same holds true for being a bitch. When bitch mode kicks into high gear, we can choose to be a reckless bitch whose destination plans are often aborted, or we can be a Responsible Bitch and produce the kind of results needed to reach our destination peacefully and on time.

It Takes a Bitch To Know z Bitch

Thanks to years of self-work, transformational training, and my academic pursuits in psychology, I believe I know myself pretty well. If you are a woman who is challenged by anger and/or emotional regulation, then I am going to take a tiny leap of faith and assert that I know you pretty well too. I come from a pedigree of reckless bitches. Truth be told, the women in my family lived daily lives ridden with challenges, stressors and threats. It would be abnormal for them to have an entire day where all went well.

I always knew my paternal grandmother, Elizabeth, to be a puffy white woman with large breasts and big arms that she would wrap around my tiny frame three times if she could. Although I never equated her packed-to-the-brim house with hoarding, I later learned it to be a symptom of the extreme depression she suffered all her life. As I will discuss in a later chapter, depression is merely anger turned inward. My maternal grandmother, Corinth was a plump black woman known for her emotional outbursts and eagerness to slap the taste out of anyone's mouth if they even looked at her wrong. Although Corinth wasn't as affectionate with me as Elizabeth, there was not a doubt in my mind that she loved me as much as she loved her baby girl, Sandra, who was also my best friend.

As a result of my grandmothers' affinity for me, they were both very protective and often kept me close to their sides. Such positioning often afforded me a clear view of the impact their reckless bitch attacks and assaults had on others. At the time, I had no idea the reckless bitch behavior exemplified by my grandmothers was covertly polishing my fangs and sharpening my razor-sharp tongue in preparation for my career as a reckless bitch. Oh, and what a career it has been.

Responsible vs. Reckless

Responsible: (adjective) morally accountable for one's behavior.

Responsible bitches res(pond) to challenges, stressors or threats after pondering.

Reckless: (adjective) acting without caring about the consequences of an action. Reckless bitches re(act) to challenges, stressors or threats after getting activated.

Bottom Line: When responding to challenges, stressors or threats, a reckless bitch is willing to drive her life into the ground to exact revenge and/or return to safety. A Responsible Bitch, on the other hand, will find a way to use the same situation to restore peace, grow from the experience, and return to safety.

Head vs. Heart

The reckless bitch allows her head to dictate her reaction. The Responsible Bitch allows her heart to inspire her response. The discrepancy here has everything to do with thinking versus feeling. For centuries, women have been taught not to trust our feelings when it comes to making important decisions. It has long been argued that trusting our feelings is the cause of irrational behavior and the absence of emotional intelligence. However, science is now busting this myth and proving that the heart has its own brain, which means it has its own form of intelligence. Research also proves that there is far more communication being transmitted from the heart-brain to the head-brain, which strongly suggests the heart-brain, is the boss of the head-brain.

What does this mean for those of us who believed that we were not supposed to use our feelings to help us navigate through some of life's most crucial decisions? It means we learned to shut our feelings off and think from our head. The unfortunate thing about thinking from our heads, especially when challenges, stressors or threats are present, is that our heads literally shut down when the going gets too tough. Physiologically speaking, when we get too hot headed, our ability to operate from the part of our brain responsible for logic and reason completely shuts down.

Unlike the brain, the heart is not designed to shut down when confronted with challenges, stressors or threats. In fact, after I teach you how to activate your heart's intelligence in the next chapter, you will see that the exact opposite holds true. When properly summoned, especially in the face of challenges, stressors or threats, the heart is ready to help guide you and all concerned to safety with peaceful solutions and resolutions.

> "We are being given a tremendous opportunity to reboot the relationship between Mind and Heart into something much more congruent and in proper alignment, where the Heart leads and the Mind simply Navigates."
>
> -Dr. Michael Lennox, Astrologer

My job as an emotion and stress regulator has been to gently reintroduce my clients to their hearts, an organ responsible for feelings, emotions and soul connections. I boldly believe, the worst thing anyone can ever do when trying to make a life-altering decision is to disregard that which they are feeling in their hearts in exchange for what they think in their heads. The following scenario perfectly demonstrates the interaction of a reckless bitch being dictated by her head and a Responsible Bitch being inspired by her heart while confronted with challenges, stressors and a threat.

Eileen Verbally Abuses Gloria, Scenario #1

Former reckless bitch, Gloria, works as a floral arranger for a very successful event coordinator by the name of Eileen. This is Gloria's dream job and she has been a dedicated employee of Eileen's for well over five years. Eileen has been in business for over fifty years. Her work is her life and she's very proud of the company she has created.

Several hours before a prestigious, televised event, Gloria and her team arrive at the venue with countless, magnificent Casablanca Lily arrangements in tow. Upon spotting the flowers, Eileen begins screaming at Gloria mercilessly while informing her that the floral selection for that particular event was supposed to be Roses, not Casablanca Lilies. Gloria stops and stiffens. Her heart rate increases. Her palms grow sweaty. She swallows hard. All these signs informing Gloria there are challenges, stressors and threats present. All eyes are now on Gloria as she attentively endures Eileen's verbal abuse and slander. Honestly, Gloria is unsure if she is actually at fault, or not. What is clear is that now is not the time to try and defend herself, unless she, too, wanted to activate the reckless bitch in her.

Gloria continued to use one of the emotion "rescue" techniques, which I will be teaching throughout this book, until Eileen's verbal storm blew over. Eventually, all hotheads run out of steam – especially if their opponent does not feed them more fuel during their eruption. Taking advantage of the first moment of silence, Gloria asked Eileen if she could step away to get to the bottom of the situation. Suggesting she do just that, Eileen cursed Gloria as she was leaving.

Remaining responsible and connected to her heart's intelligence, Gloria found and reviewed the contractual information for the event. As it turned out, Gloria was correct. The event that requested roses was for the following week. With a sigh of relief, Gloria became overwhelmed with sadness and compassion for Eileen's progressively deteriorating memory. As a reckless bitch, Gloria could have righteously stormed back into the event area, and with evidence in hand, taken her boss down, demanding that she publicly apologize to her. She could have also told her boss that she was well past retirement age and pointed to her progressively failing memory as evidence of such. This type of interaction would have been extremely detrimental to her boss and the future of her business.

Choosing to remain powerful and therefore in the Responsible Bitch mode, Gloria asked her boss if she could speak with her privately and away from where the original incident occurred. Once outside, Gloria, showed her boss the contract. Eileen's face crumbled with regret and remorse. Realizing the toll Eileen's verbal abuse had taken, Gloria made the responsible decision to request permission to go home and take care of herself emotionally. She compassionately informed Eileen that she understands the frustration of her unfortunate memory challenges and is willing to help her through it, but not at the expense of her inner peace or reputation in their industry. Clearly, Gloria destroyed nothing by choosing the Responsible Bitch route. She might have actually created a deeper bond with her boss due to her commitment to being a Responsible Bitch. Additionally, Gloria's choice to be a Responsible Bitch inevitably strengthened her confidence in her ability to regulate her emotions, control her patience, and demonstrate compassion for others during adverse situations. Pardon the pun, but it is Gloria who walked away smelling like a Rose.

Why We Get Angry

Anger: (noun) A strong feeling of displeasure, annoyance or hostility.

When confronted with the possibility of being emotionally or physically damaged, we become angry. Think of the last time someone carelessly backed out of a parking spot just as you were walking behind his or her car. Although they did not hit you, the mere fact that they could have makes you angry.

Damage + **An**ger = **DA**nger

In life, we humans are either surviving or creating. We are happiest when we are creating. If we cannot avoid **DA**nger, creating is no longer a viable option. Countless are the times I have had female clients inform me, the creative things they want to do are not possible because their daily lives are consumed with survival. As a result, they are stressed out, short-tempered and angry. It makes sense. Life experiences like this are not conducive to our happiness or wellbeing – they are **DA**ngerous.

The Brain's Watch Tower

In the area of the limbic brain, also known as the reptilian brain, we have a section called, the amygdala. The amygdala's primary accountability is to keep us from being damaged. In order to fulfill on its obsession with our safety and survival, the amygdala acts as a watchtower. It is on constant alert. The moment the amygdala senses a threat; it immediately looks to the past for familiarity and confirmation, and reacts accordingly. For example, when we get angry, the amygdala is the first to pick up on that emotion. It remembers the emotion of anger as being a precursor to damage, which signifies that danger is near.

From the moment the amygdala decides danger is near, it swiftly goes to work, preparing the best course of action for the ultimate strategic defense. The first course of action for the amygdala is to activate the release of neurotransmitters that give the body a burst of energy. This burst of energy then prepares and assists the body with its fighting or flight agenda. Next, the amygdala wakes up the big gun, a.k.a. cortisol, the stress hormone. With an "S" on its chest and a cape on its back, cortisol saturates the body's autonomic nervous system (ANS), which sends the body into a chain of reactions, all in preparation to prevent damage.

The highly evolved and intelligent prefrontal cortex of our brain is not fond of out of control cortisol surges. It considers large amounts of cortisol to be an anger to the point-of-no-return, idiot-inducing hormone, and wants nothing to do with it. Therefore, when the cortisol surge begins, the prefrontal cortex, responsible for logic and reason, logically and reasonably disengages from the craziness, leaving us at the mercy of the part of our brain responsible for instinctive behavior, domination and aggression. At this point, this primitive fight-or-flight part of our brain, coupled with the cortisol surge, takes over. In this state, it is scientifically proven that our thoughts and actions are no longer grounded in reason or logic. In other words, we are no longer in our right minds. Due to the cortisol surge, the part of the brain that bases its reactions on past experiences and, therefore, manages all challenges, stressors and threats as if we were cave women trapped in a den of hungry wolves, is now dictating us. Not only is this approach equivalent to killing a house ant with a machete, it is also the number one cause of fatal disease.

As stated earlier, my first commitment was to address the reasons why we, as women, do not chill out when we know darn well we are seconds away from irreversible damage or danger. The reason women do not chill out when we know we are in too deep is because science proves that once cortisol surges take over, the part of our brain in charge of logic, reason and that which we know to be right from wrong shuts down. So, what we know and what we are actually capable of doing become two very distinct things. We may know the right thing to do, but if the part of our brain that allows us to act logically on what we know is not available, we becomes slaves to the part of our brain that is available. In this case, only the primitive part of our brain is available. This part of our brain values survival at any cost, even if we are mistaking our nagging husband or annoying teenager for a pack of wolves or a saber tooth tiger.

More Evidence of Frontal Cortex Abandonment

Frontal cortex abandonment has everything to do with our current emotional state and our ability to regulate our emotions. Emotional regulation is most successfully managed when there is a healthy balance between the pre-frontal cortex and the amygdala. A study conducted by "Raine et al., (1998) found evidence of "decreased pre-frontal activity and increased subcortical activity (including the amygdala) in the brains of convicted murderers" (Carlson & Birknett, 2017, p. 362). These research results confirm, the amygdala is both controlled by negative emotions and it controls negative emotions. It is controlled by negative emotions because it is negative emotions that activate the amygdala in the first place. Once the amygdala is activated, it moves about producing and triggering hormones that will keep the individual tempered in such a way that he or she is prepared to attack or defend themselves by way of fight or flight while in the presence of pending danger. The hormones triggered cause the frontal cortex to disengage, placing us under the spell of our primitive brains.

Recent studies indicate women are more violent now than ever. Over the last ten years, domestic violence perpetrated by women has increased by 11%. The number of females arrested for violent crimes has risen by 40% since 2005. The amount of women losing their minds to road rage is putting men to shame. Crimes of passion are also at an all-time high (Rounds, 2015). Clearly, women know that all of these behaviors are punishable by law. Again, what women know goes out of the window when cortisol surges take over and the reckless bitch is activated. The following scenario perfectly demonstrates the behavior of a woman who is under the spell of her reptilian brain. With a slight twist of fate, this woman would have been another statistic – another convicted murderer impacted by frontal cortex abandonment. Why? Because she lost her ability to regulate her emotions.

A Pregnant Woman Hits a Man with Her Truck, Scenario #2

While shopping in Wal-Mart, Christine, a five-month pregnant woman, returned to her SUV to find a man rummaging through her purse. Yelling, she demanded he leave her property alone. Instead, he grabbed her purse and took off running. In her own words, Christine explained, "I came back out here and he was with my purse and took off and I took off after him. Me being five months pregnant, I chased him a little ways and came back, jumped in the car, threw it in gear and come across the curb and run him over. I was not letting him get away with it. It's not right, it's not fair."

Raines, the purse-snatcher was charged with larceny, breaking and entering, and property damage. The pregnant woman, Christine, is now facing serious charges of assault with a deadly weapon.

Clearly, Christine had every right to be upset. Raines rummaging through her purse and then taking off with it was a serious violation in many ways. However, the fact that Christine is now in more trouble than Raines will ever be in is a big problem that could have been avoided. It could have been avoided if Christine was able to manage her anger, interrupt her cortisol surge and prevent her reptilian brain from disengaging the part of her brain that would have enabled her to act from a place of logic and reason. There is no logic to running a person over with a car for stealing your purse. Again, when the reptilian brain takes over, it convinces you that you need a machete to kill a house ant.

Here is the other downer: for every five minutes you experience a cortisol surge, the cortisol stays in your body and continues to impact your reasoning and logic for the next twelve hours. Case and point, even after Christine ran over the man, she felt justified in doing so. She still had not come to her senses and realized that the punishment did not fit the crime. I want to reiterate, Christine had every right to be angry, without a doubt. However, by default, her reckless bitch was reactivated and she reacted, creating results that now carry serious consequences. To help you better understand what happened, I will dissect this event for you:

Christine sees a man rummaging through her purse.

Her amygdala looks to her past to determine familiarity first, proper action second.

Given Christine's reaction, chances are very good she has been stolen from before. Maybe there are also things in Christine's purse that would be very damaging to her daily life if stolen, such as medication, bankcards, etc.

Either way, the amygdala perceives imminent damage.

The amygdala confirms danger and sounds the alarm.

NOTE: Anger almost always shows up on the heels of pending danger.

Now angry and still surging cortisol, Christine's situation worsens when she demands Raines leave her purse alone and he runs off with her purse instead. The threat of damage has now magnified, causing Christine's anger to do the same. Five months pregnant Christine sprints through the parking lot, chasing after the criminal with her purse.

Christine's frontal cortex has placed her firmly in the custody of her reptilian brain because there is no longer any logic or reason to her behavior.

Unable to catch the man on foot, Christine feels the need to stop the man at any cost and therefore uses her truck to run the man over.

Christine is 100% under the possession of her reptilian brain. In addition, there are other hormones raging through her body as a result of her being pregnant.

#hormonalhotmess

Evidence that the cortisol lingers for hours after the surge is the fact that Christine then boldly admits to police and reporters what she did and why she did it, as if her actions were completely reasonable and logical. Each five-minute cortisol surge Christine experienced during this event will remain in her body for the next twelve hours, so if she was surging cortisol for ten minutes, she now has twenty-four hours of cortisol in her system. By the way, cortisol does not have a shelf life. Yes, the intensity lessens as time goes on, but it is highly likely that over the next forty-eight hours, Christine will tell that exact story several times. Like any great storyteller, in order to powerfully recreate what happened to her, Christine will most likely put herself back into the same mindset and feeling tonality as she tells the story again and again and again. What she does not know is that the brain does not distinguish between imagination and reality when it comes to the experience of sensations. This means that every time she tells the story with intensity or the same feeling tonality, her brain will assume it is happening in real time, and the cortisol surge will begin all over again - each and every time.

As I mentioned earlier, the heart is the boss of the brain. The moment the heart has a feeling the amygdala senses that feeling, deciphers it and proceeds accordingly. Here's another relevant example: think of the last time you had a heated argument with an important person in your life. During the argument, your body goes through several visceral stages including heart rate increase, sweaty palms and an unsettling feeling of nervousness. These experiences are all indications of the cortisol surging through your body. Hours later, you are still a bit unnerved, why? Because you still have cortisol sitting in your system, marinating your organs. Then at lunch, a friend says you look upset. You confirm her suspicions. You then proceed to tell her what happened verbatim, and BAM! Your heart rate increases, your palms are sweating and you are upset all over again. Why? Because you just created at least a half-day more of cortisol for your already frazzled system.

My apologies, but it gets worse, my sisters, it gets much worse. I promise you it will get better but it is important that you really know what the hell you are dealing with when you give way to your reckless bitch behavior. Hopefully, after reading this next scenario, you will understand the importance of never letting that reckless bitch peek her head into your affairs again.

A Good Woman Gone, Scenario #3

I used to have a friend that I will fictitiously refer to as, Angie. Angie and I were both program leaders at a worldwide global organization. Our job included teaching participants how to create possibilities for communities in need. In front of the room, Angie seemed like a great person. Her smile was bright and beautiful, her eyes twinkled, but at her core, she was a mean bitch. I mean, just nasty. There always seemed to be something wrong with her. She was either starting shit with someone, avoiding someone who wanted to start shit with her, or she was just plain pissed off about something. It became challenging for me and others to be with her. We simply did not know when she might get triggered and go off on us.

One day, during what I felt might be one of her calmer moments; I asked her why she was always so agitated and one breath away from cussing someone out. She told me she wasn't sure. She assured me that she had not always been that way. The sweet glisten in her eyes as she remembered who she used to be, deeply touched my heart. Digging a bit deeper, she then explained to me that she had spent most of her life angry with several family members and holding grudges longer than she should have. She then admitted that even though she was no longer upset with her family, agitation had become such a part of her life that she rarely knew any other way to be. Bottom line, living in a state of agitation was so normal for her, she forgot what normal really felt like.

Angie's reality is the reality of far too many of us women these days. Many of us have spent years and years angry and stocking up on hours, days and months worth of cortisol. Because cortisol does not have a shelf life, it hangs out in our system until its time is up. As a result, we become so drenched with cortisol, that the experience of being stressed and easily agitated becomes our norm. Angie admitted to me that people from her past often ask her what happened because she used to be a kind, peaceful, level-headed person. Angie did not know how to answer that question because she was not aware that her personality shift was the direct effect of stress and specifically being overstocked with the stress hormone, cortisol. Here's the very sad part of the story: Angie was eventually diagnosed with a very aggressive form of cancer, and unfortunately the cancer had spread throughout her entire body, primarily attacking her organs. Angie did not survive. The day Angie passed away, one of her close friends called me to give me the news. She was quick to tell me, "Sadly, most of you only knew Angie as a bridge burner and personality arsonist, but she wasn't always that way." I do not believe cancer killed Angie. I believe Angie's anger killed Angie.

You see, during primitive times, when faced with a challenge, stressor or threat, we needed the stress hormone cortisol to help us get away from the saber tooth tiger nipping at our heels. Back then; we humans were mostly on foot so the five minutes of cortisol surge gave us twelve hours of strength and endurance to run the distance needed to safety. However, the challenges, stressors and threats that stimulate cortisol surges today do not require the physical endurance we needed as primates. For the most part, when angered or upset, we sit and stew and as we do, the avalanche of cortisol sits too. The nowhere to go or no way to burn off cortisol sits in our system, stressing out our organs, causing dis-ease.

> NOTE: Prominent signs of cortisol overload include excess abdominal fat, insomnia, fatigue, weight gain, mood swings, puffy face and anxiety.

So, what's the solution? Should we try living a life free of the anger as to not alert the amygdala in the first place? Is that realistic? Is it even possible? Perhaps if we are living as Monks in the Himalayas it might be. However, given our reality, I think it is absolutely unreasonable to believe we can set our lives up to never ever be angry again. Sure, we can attempt to better regulate our anger and even alter our relationship to anger, as I will explain in chapter four. ~~However,~~ Crucial is the fact that we are physiologically, emotionally, physically and psychologically hijacked by cortisol surges. The logic is inescapable. If we can interrupt cortisol surges, then we can prevent the frontal cortex from leaving us in the custody of our primitive brain that equates all danger with that of a saber tooth tiger.

So, is it even possible to interrupt this cortisol surge? Thanks to several techniques I have discovered or created it is absolutely possible to interrupt this stress hormone and organically restore peace. Even better news; by the end of this book not only will you be able to dodge that cortisol bullet, like Neo in the Matrix, you won't have to. You will have all the information you need to be someone who can responsibly and peacefully handle *all* things – especially your anger.

Dr. Bernie Siegel, an alternative medicine physician, wrote one of my all-time favorite books in 1984 called "Love, Medicine and Miracles." In the book, Dr. Siegel shared the story of a cancer patient who had undergone a double mastectomy. When asked how she felt post-surgery, she replied, "I feel as though I just got a lot off my chest" (Siegal, 1984). A lot of what? You guessed, it – a lot of repressed anger that eventually expressed itself in the form of cancer.

The first point I want to make about anger is that anger is not always expressed in an explosive manner such as in Angie's case. The second point is, anger, be it suppressed or expressed, creates stress hormones that are toxic and can lead to deadly diseases. The third point I want to make is, anger is an emotion that must be in motion. When we can shift our response towards anger from reckless to responsible by regulating our cortisol, *dis*-ease returns to ease and peace becomes our daily experience – regardless of the circumstances.

"My own day to day clinical experiences have convinced

me that the state of the mind changes the state of the body by working through the central nervous system, the endocrine system, and the immune system. Peace of mind sends the body a 'live' message, while depression, fear, and unresolved conflict give it a 'die' message."

–Dr. Bernie Siegel, Love, Medicine & Miracles

CHAPTER 3
OWNING YOUR UGLY

The Heart Rules

The great news about the heart being the boss of the head is that most of us women are naturally inclined to be inspired by our hearts rather than our heads when it comes to making decisions. In other words, it is typical to hear a woman say, "I feel this, therefore, I think this." That being said, being a Responsible Bitch has everything to do with being able to recognize a trigger or bitch button activation fast enough to allow our heart's intelligence to guide us, as opposed to our progressively hot growing head. Here is a perfect example of how turning to the heart alters everything when a challenge, stressor, or threat manages to emotionally snag you:

Finding the Pretty in the Panic, Scenario #4

Recently, I found myself running late for an eyebrow trimming appointment. The lady that does my brows has a tight schedule, and when my thirty minutes are up, finished or not, she wants me out of her chair so she can be on time for her next client. Trust me, leaving with only one brow done because I was late is no fun. I pull into the back lot, praying my parking unicorn has answered my prayer. Sure enough, every spot is full but there is one car pulling out. "Yes, Thank you!" I scream to my parking unicorn that never lets me down.

As the woman's brake lights illuminate, I wait patiently for her to pull out. She stops, checks her rear-view mirror and slowly lets her car roll out of the spot. "Oh, Jeez!" I immediately said out loud. Instantly, I felt my heart rate starting to increase and my breathing grew shallow. "Oh, shit! I'm getting pissed off," I said to myself. But then, in that split second, I used one of my favorite emotional rescue techniques that quickly connected me to my heart. I recognized that I had been triggered and by immediately implementing the technique, my perspective of the woman instantly changed. I looked at the woman again. By this time, her car had slowly rolled halfway out of my future parking spot. In my current state of coherence, I was better able to understand what was going on. You see, my trigger is deception. When I pulled into the parking lot and saw her break lights go on, I assumed she would be quickly pulling out of the spot so I could just as fast pull in. However, because it took longer than expected, I was triggered, I felt deceived.

Re-examining the situation from my heart's perspective, made the situation make sense to me. The woman was only using her rear-view mirror as visual guidance for fear that if she turned around and looked too far over her shoulder, she might mess her beautiful new hair-do up. Furthermore, while using her rear-view mirror for guidance she happened to like what she was seeing in the reflection and was splitting her time between backing out of the parking spot and admiring herself and her new hair-do. Can I just say, major heart swell! In a split second, I saw me at her age and I fell madly in love with her. How wonderful it is, I thought, that at her age she is still holding it down, hair done, nails done, everything looking good. I watched with a proud smile on my face and tears glistening my eyes as Madam Gorgeousness continued to appreciate herself while slowly relinquishing my future parking spot.

With practice comes perfection. Soon, with a little practice and a commitment to being responsible for your bitchiness, you will know exactly how to keep that reckless bitch at bay. As much as I hate to admit this, the old me would have laid heavily on the horn, scaring the crap out of that old lady, causing her to have a cortisol surge and perhaps even a heart attack. With twelve hours of cortisol flowing through her frail and fragile frame, her whole day would have been knocked off kilter and the Gorgeous Madam would also be a trembling mess. Instead, she eventually drove out of the lot feeling perfect and pretty. Not to get too dramatic here, but who knows how many of those visits are really left in her lifetime? What if that was her last visit to the beauty salon that she has probably frequented most of her life? Do I really want to be the reckless bitch that messed it up for her with my anger and impatience? No, I think not. I doubt she even noticed me through it all, but I noticed her. I was very grateful for the view, and experiences like that are indeed worth one untrimmed brow.

Now, before I teach you one my favorite emotion regulation techniques that I use, and millions of others use, including NASA, Hospitals, Police Departments, PTSD vets and more, I think it is important for us to first distinguish and then understand what exactly pisses you off in the first place. Distinguishing this information about yourself can be far more powerful than any emotion regulation tool or tip I teach you, because it will put you at the source of your emotions. Being at the source is far more powerful because you will be able to destroy your potential upsets by pulling them out by the root as opposed to later dealing with your anger as a symptom.

The Birth of Your Trigger

I want to briefly revisit the scenario of the pregnant woman, Christine, who hit the man with her truck as depicted in chapter two. When interviewed by the police and reporters, Christine boldly declared, "I wasn't letting him get away with it. It's not right. It's not fair." Can you guess what Christine's trigger is? She states it clear as day. This five-month pregnant woman put her safety and the safety of her unborn child in danger the moment she felt an injustice was being done to her. Again, her exact words were, "it's not right. It's not fair." Christine's trigger is, injustice. Here is the irony, it is the threat of damage and the fight or flight for survival that activates the reptilian brain in the first place. However, once activated, we often put ourselves in more danger and do more damage than the original threat of damage could have ever done. It makes no sense at all. The reptilian brain never does.

As I mentioned, my trigger is deception. All triggers are born from an original incident in which we experience grief. In other words, something unbelievable happens to us for the first time, which is why it is referred to as the original incident. That experience then causes us great sadness and as we mature and decide against being vulnerable, we mask our sadness with the third stage of grief, which is anger. My original incident occurred when I was four-years-old and I had that frustrating experience on Sesame Street with Kermit the Frog. That experience was the first of many deceptive experiences life seemed to have in store for me. Unfortunately, once we develop our trigger, by default, circumstances and situations will find us in order to deepen our sensitivity to our triggers. I will go into further detail about that later. For now, here are two examples of how my trigger continued to wiggle its wicked way into my life. When I was five years old, I told my mother that a close family friend was doing things to me in my bed at night that I did not like. I was certain she was going to make him stop and protect me from future violations. Instead she called me a liar and refused to confront him. At that time, I did not know my biological father so my mother was my everything. I believed my mother's job was to protect me and keep me safe. Initially, her unwillingness to do either, shocked me. Later, I remember being extremely sad because she was not the Mother I believed she should be. I felt deceived. I decided I would have to learn how to protect myself.

At the age of seven, I convinced my mother to let me join the neighborhood martial arts training team for kids. The program was called The Chelsea Infants. The man who taught the self-defense program was a large, heavyset man with a kind smile. I believed him when he promised me that he would teach me how to defend myself against bad men, bigger than him. Unfortunately, he turned out to be a child molester. He was molesting all of the girls and boys on the team. He convinced us girls that earning our belt ranks in karate was no different than how we could move up the corporate ladder in the world. He told us, the more sexual favors we could do for men, the stronger and more powerful we would be. More deception. The martial arts teacher who was supposed to teach me how to protect myself from sexual predators and other threats turned out to be my biggest threat of all. As I mentioned, as a young girl, my life was drenched with deception. From having to deceive Sesame Street viewers into believing I did not know how to tie my shoes, to joining a beautiful religion that I later learned advocated for me to become a child-bride.

Identifying Your Trigger Exercise

By now, you might know exactly what your trigger is, you might have an idea of what your trigger is, or you might not have the slightest clue. If you think you know what your trigger is, or if you are certain you know what your trigger is, I request that you forget what you know or think you know. Letting go for a little while will allow us to see if perhaps there is a deeper cut of your trigger ready to reveal itself to you. The intention of this exercise is to help you get to the originating incident of your trigger and then we will assign a name and an experience to your trigger. Okay, let's get started. Please sit or lay in a comfortable, quiet space. Closing your eyes, I want you to see if you can remember the first time you experienced extreme sadness. This incident usually occurs somewhere between the ages of four and eight years of age, and it likely caused you much grief. If you think you remember the incident, what was the experience the sadness left you with? For instance, my incident left me with the experience of being deceived. Here are several other common experiences that might ring a bell for you:

Abandonment, belittled, blame, bossiness, change of plans, contempt, cowardliness, criticized, deceived, disillusioned, disrespected, dominating, false accusations, guilt, hindered, ignored, inadequacy, inferior, injustice, interrupted, impatience, isolated, powerless, rejection, sarcasm, shame, suspicious, teased, trapped, undermined.

Granted, most of these triggers could apply to us all because there are obviously a series of experiences that can be upsetting. However, there is one particular trigger that has the potential to consistently and swiftly send you into a full-blown anger and/or rage. Below is an example of how one of my current client's trigger is rooted in her originating incident:

Katie's Story, Scenario #5

When Katie was five years old, her parents left her in China with her grandmother as they traveled to the United States to create a new life for their family. Although Katie loved her grandmother very much, her grandmother was an elderly lady and was not able to do a lot of the fun things Katie remembered doing with her mother. Longing to be with her mother again, Katie slept with her mother's pictures under her pillow and would talk to her mother's photos every night. She promised her mother that when she was with her again, she would never leave her side. Two years later, at the age of seven, Katie moved to the states to be with her parents. Keeping her promise, she spent every moment she could by her mother's side. Like a loyal puppy, Katie would follow her mother from room to room, relishing her scent, her beauty, the way she walked, the movement of her hair when her mother walked, all of it. She admits she was madly in love with her mother.

At first, Katie's mother seemed okay with her only daughter shadowing her every move. However, one day, right before Katie's 8th birthday she remembers following her mother around the house, as she always did, when her mother skid to an abrupt stop. Pivoting on her heels and looking down at Katie she then angrily asked, "Katie, why must you follow me everywhere I go all the time, what is wrong with you?" Stunned by her mother's behavior, Katie responded, "I just love you and want to be with you all the time." Katie's mom then responded, "you cannot be with me all the time! We live in the same house and that should be enough for you because I do not want to be with you all the time, now go and learn how to be on your own, it's just not healthy!" Crying even harder, Katie remembers running away emotionally shattered. The thing about the originating incident for which our triggers are born, is that it doesn't matter who is right or who is wrong. In Katie's case, in many ways her mother had a very valid point. Katie's attachment was becoming unhealthy for both of them. However, when you take right and wrong out of the equation all that is left is the upsetting experience that leads to the birth of the trigger that later becomes the impetus for the anger.

Professionally, Katie works as an intensive care unit Nurse. She came to our program because she had been arrested for spousal abuse. The Judge sentenced her to 52-weeks of Anger Management. The incident that led to Katie's arrest had to do with her ex-husband at the time, Robert, and his desire to have extramarital affairs. Robert explained to Katie, for the sake of their daughters, he was willing to live in the same house with her but he no longer wanted to be with her romantically. Within seconds, Katie lost her temper and told him that he would not be allowed to live in the same house with her if he was not willing to be with her. Mind you, Katie's original incident with her mother was almost identical to this experience with her husband. Once again, someone Katie loved was informing her, they were willing to stay in the same house with her but they did not want to be with her. When Katie finally calmed down, she convinced Robert to allow her to be a part of his flings and if he were willing to do so, she would allow him to remain in their home. Robert begrudgingly agreed.

Robert and Katie participated in ménage à trois sex with a woman by the name of Sabrina for several weeks and all seemed to be going well. However, Katie's life changed forever the day she came home to find Sabrina and Robert in bed having sex. Visibly upset, Katie reminded Robert that sex with Sabrina was something they were supposed to be doing together. At that point, Robert informed Katie, he simply did not want to be with her. Sabrina echoed Robert's words verbatim. In a matter of seconds, Katie was on her way to reckless bitch hell in a handbasket. When she ran out of items to throw at the naked and terrified Robert and Sabrina, she jumped on top of Robert and continued to smack, punch, bite and pull his hair. In a panic, Sabrina called 911. Completely disengaged from her frontal cortex brain, Katie's cortisol surge activated her reptilian brain causing her to behave like a wild animal until the police arrived.

Katie's behavior perfectly exemplifies the power our triggers have over us. It is also important to note that anger does not discriminate. Even the most dedicated yogis have emotional challenges that include anger. When it comes to being a Responsible Bitch, I consider myself a pro. I also go through extreme measures to avoid putting myself in a space or place that I might potentially be triggered. Yet, once in a while, that little trigger sneaks right up on me and before you know it, I'm emotionally unraveling like the snag on a crocheted sweater. Case and point, my initial reaction to Madam Gorgeousness.

Identifying Your Bitch Buttons & Protecting Them

When I think of my triggers and my buttons and the differences between the two, I think of the electrical breaker panel in my condo. It's a simple panel on the wall, and when you open it, you will see two distinct things. Typically, you will see side by side, vertical rows of switches that can be turned on and off. These switches can control the electric activity to specific rooms and appliances in my home. Near the rows of switches, you will find the main breaker, which is a large double switch that has the power to shut down the entire electrical system in my home with one flick of the switch. Plain and simple, I regard the main breaker as my trigger, something that has the absolute power to shut me down. I view the vertical rows of switches, as my bitch buttons. Much like the switches, these bitch buttons can control specific feelings and emotions when pushed, but they do not have a natural power, like my trigger, to shut me down. However, it is possible to activate the reckless bitch when and if these bitch buttons are continuously pushed to the extent that it reaches tolerance capacity and therefore enables the "breaker-panel" trigger. The following scenario exemplifies how bitch buttons are born and what we can do to protect our bitch buttons from being pushed.

Do Your Own Damn Dishes, Scenario #6

Jennifer was the oldest of three children being raised by their single father. Jennifer's father worked but was often barely able to make ends meet. In spite of their financial challenges that prevented them from eating at nice restaurants, Jennifer's father was committed to creating a well-developed palette for his children. He did precisely that by preparing tasty meals for his family just about every night. According to Jennifer, her father was a messy cook, and he used just about every dish and pot he could find in the kitchen when cooking. Unfortunately, Jennifer's father designated her to be the family dishwasher. Growing up, it bothered her deeply that her siblings could not at the very least was their dish. Needless to say, as an adult, Jennifer's bitch button is activated whenever anyone leaves a single dish in her sink, with the expectation that she will wash it.

After working with Jennifer, she and I were able to put

several structures in place to protect her from bitch button activation. These structures include the use of paper plates for her children, reducing her children's allowance when a dish is left in the sink instead of loading it into the dishwasher, and when Jennifer has visitors over, she politely informs her guest of her zero tolerance for dishes left in the sink. To date, Jennifer has only had to ask one houseguest to go for failure to comply. Jennifer's husband is incredibly committed to protecting Jennifer's bitch buttons and in turn, she protects and honors his dick buttons – but that's another book.

Emotion Regulation Technique #1 – Quick Coherence®

Knowing the triggers, buttons and the techniques I will teach you only work if you are willing to make the conscious effort to make them work. Even then, there will be times that you will not be able to avoid the experience of anger. However, you will have the knowledge and the ability to diminish the duration of your anger and the impact it has on your body. The first emotion regulation technique I will teach you is called Quick Coherence ® Created by The Institute of HeartMath™. The intention of this particular technique is to support you in maintaining coherence when presented with challenges, stressors or threats. According to The Institute of HeartMath™:

"There are times when we have experienced being in sync and flowing with a sense of ease through daily challenges. When we are in a coherent flow, things that come up don't seem to get under our skin. We achieve coherence when the heart, mind, emotions, and body are all working in sync. We are then able to "take charge" of ourselves and maintain our composure. We have more energy, time seems to pass by quickly and we seem to flow through or around issues. When challenges come up, we can think more clearly, handle a situation and move on. We have increased energy and stability."

--HeartMath™Institute

By establishing a state of coherence, we can immediately interrupt the biochemical activity that occurs during challenges, stressors or threats. This Quick Coherence ® technique is by far my favorite and I use it all the time, especially when people are yelling in my face at work. Remember, I work with women who are working on their anger issues and sometimes my response to their behavior triggers them and I have to deal with the consequences. What I like so much about this technique is that it works in a matter of seconds and no one has to know you are doing it. It is a simple, personal experience that provides you with enormous power.

Although the chances are very good that you will be using this technique when you are standing, walking, driving or mobile in some way, I'd like you to learn this technique while you are sitting comfortably. I'll guide you through the two primary steps involved below. Earlier, I told you that science has proven that our hearts have a brain. What this technique is going to do, is teach you how to activate your heart's intelligence. When we are able to activate our hearts intelligence in the face of challenges, threats or stressors, we can completely disengage from our brain and rely solely on the intelligence of our hearts. The intelligence of our hearts, as I mentioned earlier, will never abandon us when the going gets tough.

Step One – Activating Your Heart's Intelligence

It is very important that you learn how to master the

execution of this technique with your eyes open. Why? Because when you are presented with a challenge a stress or threat the last thing you want to do is close your eyes. So find a spot in the room and just relax your open eyes on that spot. Now I would like you to pretend that your heart has nostrils. If you need to use your right hand to draw imaginary nostrils over the heart area, please do so. Now, with your eyes resting softly on that spot, I would like you to breathe through your hearts nostrils for five seconds in and eight seconds out, at a pace that feels comfortable for you. Please practice this breathing process for one full minute.

Step Two – Creating A Regenerative Feeling

As you continue breathing through your heart's nostrils, five seconds in and eight seconds out, at a pace that is comfortable for you, I would like you to think of a time in your life in which you were overwhelmed with the experience of compassion or gratitude. Once you have connected with the feeling tonality of compassion and or gratitude, I would like you to allow that feeling tonality to drench your heart. As you start to relish this beautiful space, please continue to breathe five seconds in and eight seconds out, through your heart's nostrils, at a pace that is comfortable to you. Please continue this step for one full minute.

Example: The feeling tonality of gratitude and compassion that I use during this step is remembering the first time I saw my son's face after giving birth. The memory overwhelms me with compassion and gratitude. I take that feeling tonality and I immerse my heart in it as I continue to breathe five seconds in and eight seconds out, at a pace that feels comfortable to me.

If you were able to complete these two steps correctly, at this point you should be feeling a wonderful sense of lightness, peace and ease. If you do not feel any difference at all, please be patient. This is a technique that you could easily master with practice. For the sake of teaching you this technique, I will assume you did both steps as they were designed to be done and are now experiencing a state of lightness, peace and ease. That being said, I want to congratulate you on activating your heart's intelligence and consciously creating your first Dehydroepiandrosterone (DHEA) surge.

The reason that this technique is so powerful is because your ability to activate your heart's intelligence simultaneously enables you to activate the vitality hormone DHEA. Just like activating your reptilian brain enables you to activate the stress hormone cortisol. DHEA is an antagonist to cortisol. So, what does that mean in layman's terms? When we are activating the stress hormone cortisol during a challenge, stressor or threat we are heading towards reckless bitch territory. When we are activating the DHEA vitality hormone during a challenge, stressor or threat we are heading towards Responsible Bitch territory. Yes, if you are able to simply breathe five seconds in and eight seconds out through your heart while allowing a feeling of compassion or gratitude to overwhelm you, your experience of reckless bitch behavior is over.

When I realized interrupting my cortisol surge was a possibility, I could not help but to say, "this is some good shit, man!" But if you are like me, you might be wondering, what happens if my challenge, stressor or threat is far more overwhelming than any past memory of gratitude or compassion that I am able to draw upon in the moment? Or, what if I'm too paralyzed by fear to regulate my breath? What do I then? These are important questions and the answers to these questions is why this technique works so well. You see, regardless of the situation you are in, the one thing you will be doing, if nothing else, is breathing. If you are not breathing, chances are you are dead.

My point is, if you can breathe, you can use this technique. During a challenging situation, you may not be able to breathe five seconds in or eight seconds out at a pace that is comfortable for you; I got that. However, what you can do is intentionally shift your breathing from your head to your heart. It is that easy. When you consciously choose to breathe from your heart, you activate your heart's intelligence. This small shift will then immediately alter your Heart Rate Variability (HRV) and keep you from slipping into the aggressive arms of your reptilian brain and turning into a reckless bitch. In my HeartMath (TM) workshops, using a volunteer from the audience and a device known as EMWave Pro(TM) I can demonstrate, live and on a big screen how easy and effective this simple shift to heart breathing from head breathing works.

Okay, my fabulously coherent sisters, a.ka. Responsibly Powerful Bitches, before we move on, please take a few minutes to fill in the following information for your future reference. Please note, the information you add below regarding your original incident and triggers may or may not change, and that is okay. We must learn to look at our emotional life like an onion. The more we work on ourselves, the more layers we are able to peel away, bringing us closer to our core.

My original incident was:

My trigger is:

My buttons are:

My rejuvenating feelings come from my memories of:

(Please list at least 3 memories in which you were overwhelmed with compassion or gratitude. You will want to continue adding to this list and keep these memories at the forefront of your mind for easy access when confronted with a challenge, stressor or threat.)

It is my sincere hope that at this point, you have a pretty good idea of your triggers and buttons that piss you off and why. I trust that you now understand why controlling the reckless bitch in you is very difficult once she is activated but it is no longer impossible. And, no matter what, the good news is you now have access to a vitality hormone generating technique that can help you keep your cool when the world around you is acting a fool. I would also like to acknowledge you for your willingness to identify and be responsible for the trigger and buttons that constitutes the bitch in you.

Distinguishing the origin of our ugly and owning our ugly can be an uncomfortable and daunting endeavor. However, when we can fall madly in love with ourselves for everything we are and everything we are not, what immediately follows is a proud sense of ownership of self. The more we can accept and own all of our negative and positive traits, the more space we have for others. The more space we have for others, the less challenged, threatened or stressed we will be by them. Thus, a line is drawn in the sand. Their stuff is their stuff, and our stuff belongs to us.

CHAPTER 4
YOU MAKE YOU WELL

The 411 On Dis-Ease

We women often justify becoming reckless bitches and losing our marbles when rightfully defending ourselves or justifiably exacting revenge. Truth be told, my beautiful sisters, even when we are in the right, each time we give way to the reckless bitch, what we are really doing is swallowing the poison with the hope that the other person dies. Of course, on some level we know this, which is why it is not uncommon, during a cortisol surge, for us to spew the words, "you make me sick!" at our opponents. We know. We women always know. Now we just have to make sure that we make powerful choices with all that we know. Powerful choices include living our lives as Responsible Bitches and keeping ourselves well.

It is always worth mentioning, I am in no way saying we should never be angry. I am also not implying that we should never be stressed out. Neither would be realistic. The fact of the matter is, anger caused by stress is as much a part of life as the common cold. Although stress-induced anger does not discriminate, it does play favorites. Like water to fish, there is a population in which stress-induced anger has reportedly become an epidemic. Can you guess the demographic of this population? Of course you can! Stress and stress-induced anger seems to be particularly fond of us women.

If I may speak on behalf of my league, I feel that we women have come to terms with the fact that we have to do it all or most of it all. Doing it all or most of it all leaves us feeling overwhelmed, stressed out and tired. If and when you stand on our last nerve in those moments of exhaustion, trust me, it will be your last step for a while because we will take you down.

In addition to having to do it all or most of it all, women are now performing many of the same tasks as men, yet the expectations of us are higher. That's enough injustice to piss anyone off. No one expects little Bobby's single dad to bring him to school looking as if he just stepped off the pages of a kid's clothing line catalog. On the flip side, if it was Bobby's mom dropping him off and she brought him to school looking like an unmade bed, heads would turn and her back would blister from the contemptuous glares. I could go on and on explaining why stress-induced anger favors us hard-working, dedicated, committed, tireless, passionate, nurturing, kick ass, take charge women, but I have never been one to focus on the problem. Responsibly Powerful Bitches are all about the solution!

Our Health Is In Our Hearts

Due to specific biochemical activity, our hearts have a very strong connection to anger. When we are angry, specific neurotransmitters constrict our blood vessels, and our hearts go from pumping one gallon of blood per minute to pumping five gallons of blood per minute. This means, our anger causes our hearts to work harder and faster than they should. After several years of these reckless bitch induced demands on our hearts, it is easy to see how and why chronic anger can lead to fatal heart diseases such as high blood pressure, heart attacks, and strokes. Let's not forget, when we are in the reckless bitch mode there is also damage being done to us by the overflow of cortisol. Too much cortisol in our already taxed organs lead to Cushing's disease, cancer, and damage to our nervous, immune, metabolic, cardiovascular and digestive systems.

Our health is also in our hearts because it is our feelings that are the real manifestations of our reality. If you feel that you are sick all the time, you will eventually start thinking you're sick all the time and ultimately, you *will* be sick all the time. Everything starts in our hearts as a feeling tonality, then we formulate thoughts that become things. I believe this is why many Physicians and clinical researchers often contract the diseases that they are studying. These scientists invest so much time feeling certain emotions about their hypothesis or the disease itself - be it anger or deep appreciation - that emotional feeling tonality creates thoughts, and ultimately, thoughts create reality. In a nutshell, as your heart feels, your life and body reveal.

> "Stress is a pervasive phenomenon, not only for one's work-life but life in general. It is also the biggest challenge to achieving psychological health."
>
> -P. Muchinsky & S. Culbertson

Keeping Your Emotions in Motion

So, what is the solution? If we cannot avoid stress, or even worse, stress-induced anger, what is a Responsible Bitch to do when it comes to making herself well? The best thing that we can do to protect ourselves from the damage of toxic energy is to provide an outlet for the unwanted emotions, such as anger, to flow through us and out of us. This concept is easier to grasp if you think of emotions as a form of energy. All energy needs a clear circuit to travel through, otherwise, it gets stopped and stuck and eventually short circuits. The same holds true for toxic emotions. If there is no clear channel or outlet for them to travel through, the emotion stops or gets stuck. Once the toxic emotion is stopped or stuck, toxins are eventually released into that area. Upon release, the toxins contaminate the area, infecting the tissues, cell membranes, and other body parts. This creates discomfort and eventually disease. Distinguishing the channel or the physical platform for your toxic emotional release is an easy process. The trick is to match the physical action or activity that shouts for you when your reckless bitch is activated. I then advise my clients to participate in that physical action or activity at least twice a week to ensure their emotional outlet channels remain clear and unclogged.

Elma the Fighter, Scenario #7

Elma's anger issues stem from her in-utero experience. Elma's mother was five months pregnant with Elma when her husband, Elma's father, died suddenly. Elma's mother went through a kaleidoscope of emotions after her husband's death. Research proves a fetus feels and experiences the emotional state of the mother. The primary emotion Elma's mother admitted to feeling after losing her husband was anger. Now at the age of twenty-eight, Elma is challenged by deep-rooted anger issues that activate the reckless bitch in her whenever she feels trapped or stuck. When I asked Elma what physical activity her reckless bitch yearned for to express her anger, she informed me she wanted to fight. When I asked her what she wanted to fight with, she explained she wanted to kick her way out of the constricted space that angered her. The space that she was referring to was her original home, inside her mother's womb where the uterus walls were lined with anger.

It quickly became obvious to me that the physical activity best suited for Elma would be kickboxing or Krav Maga, the military self-defense system that teaches people how to fight their way out of tight holds in realistic situations. Elma believes her participation in Kickboxing has drastically reduced the length of her bitch button activations, completely removed her trigger activation, and she sleeps better at night. Intuitively, we usually have an idea of the physical platform that would best serve our emotional outlet needs. But just in case, here are some physical activities that might best suit you. When your reckless bitch is activated and all you want to do is argue to no end, I highly recommend that you join a debate team. If you feel the need to run when your reckless bitch is activated, I highly recommend that you do exactly that. However, do it on a treadmill, while listening to your idea of powerful and aggressive music. If you are someone who tends to hide, aerial yoga would be wonderful for you because it gives you the opportunity to hide in the yoga silk while peaking at the world from a variety of safe perspectives. By the way, it is perfectly fine if crying is the physical activity you normally use to move your emotions. My only suggestion is that you opt for tears of joy over tears of sadness to prevent unexpected cortisol surges.

If none of the above physical activities feel like adequate physical forms of expression for your reckless bitch energy to flow through, then I suggest you give hot yoga a try. Hot Yoga is a practice that was initially derived from the ninety-minute practice of Bikram Yoga and based on the twenty-six postures designed to detox, restore, and repair the body's organs in a room heated to 105 degrees Fahrenheit or higher. I now practice core power yoga because I feel the core power yoga does a great job incorporating my mind and my body during my practice. I love how each posture I move into with my body informs me of what is going on in my mind. In the most wonderful way, each posture represents a thought process. If the posture I am practicing is off, chances are, the thought that reflects that particular posture is also off. What's even more amazing is that when I am unable to get to the root of that particular thought, for whatever reason, by simply mastering the posture affiliated with that thought, peace regarding that thought instantly follows. I recall many times where I stepped onto to my yoga mat confused and stepped off my yoga mat forty-five minutes later with a crystal clear mind.

Peace Sleep

I did not come to appreciate the health benefits of sleep until I got serious about regulating my emotions. It was then that I also learned, sleep also plays a large role when it comes to losing weight. I actually took sleep for granted. I would even joke around and say, "who needs sleep? I will sleep when I am dead." When my family physician informed me that my weight plateau was most likely due to sleep deficiency I did not believe him. After conducting my own research, I was stunned to learn, sleep deprivation increases cortisol levels. According to sleep specialist Dr. Breus, author of *The Sleep Doctor's Diet Plan: Lose Weight Through Better Sleep*, if we rob ourselves of a measly thirty minutes of sleep, we increase our chances of unwanted weight gain (Michael, 2011). The following results reported by a study conducted by Annals of Internal Medicine sums up the impact sleep deprivation has on weight extremely well.

> "When you're sleep deprived, the mitochondria in your cells that digest fuel start to shut down. Sugar remains in your blood and you end up with high blood sugar. Losing out on sleep can make fat cells 30 percent less able to deal with insulin.
> --*Annals of Internal Medicine*

Psychologically, sleep is also as important because it allows us to check out of our conscious reality and into the realm of our psyche and unconscious minds. This time out gives us time away from the arduous task of conscious thinking, evaluating and assessing. Carl Jung speaks at length about the importance of the unconscious mind as it pertains to establishing psychological balance. According to Jung, the psyche is always seeking to find balance between the conscious and the unconscious mind. In his book, "The Archetypes and the Collective Unconscious," Jung wrote, "dreams contain fantasies which 'want' to become conscious." He continues, "The sources of dreams are often repressed instincts which have a natural tendency to influence the conscious mind" (Jung, 1990. p. 60). More often than not, the information necessary to establish this balance is more than our conscious minds can handle during our waking state. So, when we go to sleep, our subconscious mind steps in to compensate for what our conscious mind is not capable of handling during the day. This compensatory effect between our conscious and unconscious mind is why some people have nightmares or dreams that are weird and out of this world. That is our psyche at work, processing the shit in our head at night so our conscious mind feels whole and complete during the day. If we are not sleeping long enough to allow this psychological compensatory process to take place, we are robbing ourselves of our own peace of mind and laying fertile soil for the activation and growth of our reckless bitch.

Although I personally found the physical and psychological reasons for a peaceful night's sleep inspiring in their own right, understanding the physiology of sleep granted me the opportunity to approach sleep from a responsible perspective. What I did not know and what I am excited to share with those of you also not in the know, is that there are four main stages of sleep. It is crucial that each stage be fully experienced because the stages are linear and collectively, the four stages make up one sleep cycle. Each cycle occurs approximately within a ninety-minute time frame.

During a normal night of sleep, most people will cycle through four or five of these cycles prior to awakening which totals six or seven hours of sleep. The first stage is known as non-Rem which is short for non-rapid eye movement (NREM). During this stage we often find ourselves straddling sleep and wakefulness. It is also during this stage that we may experience hypnagogic hallucinations in which we hear or see things that are not located in reality. We may experience ourselves falling, or may have muscle jerks. This sensation is known as hypnic jerks and is most often experienced by individuals with irregular sleep patterns.

The second stage is also NREM sleep, however unlike stage one, this stage includes a deeper sleep, making it harder for us to be awakened. This stage is important because it is believed to be a cortisol arousal suppressor. By suppressing cortisol in this stage, we are then better able to move into the next stage of sleep, known as slow wave sleep. Women with large amounts of cortisol in their system find this sleep stage the most challenging to push through. Tossing and turning during this phase, due to cortisol arousal, is frustrating and it prevents one from effortlessly reaching the slow wave sleep we all yearn for.

The slow wave sleep is the third stage of sleep and it is the last non-Rem stage. During this stage, the sleep is extremely deep, making it very difficult to awaken. This is also the stage in which behaviors such as sleep-walking and sleep-talking occur. Attempting to awaken anyone during this stage is often very difficult.

The fourth sleep stage is known as the rapid eye

movement stage (REM). It is during this stage that our eyes are rapidly moving beneath our closed lids. In contrast to the rapid movement of the eyes, for the most part the entire body is motionless due to a form of muscular paralysis. It is also during this stage that dreaming occurs. It has been suggested that the dream state and the temporary paralysis stage happen simultaneously to prevent people from physically reacting to their dreams. Significant alterations during this stage would interfere with the individual's dream state. And, as I mentioned earlier, dream states are crucial to the formation of our psychological balance. Additionally, REM is believed to be a restorative state. Without the full restorative experiences, our awakened state might be riddled with fatigue, brain fog and the experience of being agitated – all of which can contribute to reckless bitch behavior. The bottom line is, sleep is what provides our bodies with the down time we need to regenerate cells, muscles, and tissues while keeping us psychologically sound and physically fabulous.

The last thing I want to say about sleep is directed to those of you who have trouble falling asleep at night. Like you, I used to toss and turn for hours before awakening to daylight. According to researchers at www.sleepfoundation.org, insomnia is caused by your brain's desire to remain in the awakened state cycle as opposed to switching to the sleep cycle. I am sure you will not be surprised to know that stress plays a big part in the brain's choice to remain awake. At this point, you should also know, when stress is factored in as the cause of an experience, unhealthy levels of the stress hormone cortisol are not too far behind. The good news is that we now know how to interrupt cortisol surges organically. We also know how to replace cortisol with the vitality hormone DHEA. So, what this means is we can now responsibly put ourselves to sleep instead of recklessly tossing and turning all night.

Insomnia Exercises

Step #1 Capacitar Finger Positions

While relaxing in your favorite sleeping position, press your right index and middle finger against your forehead and press your left index and middle finger on your chest, in the space between your breasts.

Step #2 Heart Focus Breathing

With your fingers gently pressing your forehead and your chest area, begin breathing through your heart's nostrils; five seconds in and eight seconds out at a pace that feels comfortable for you.

Not only will this process put you to sleep quickly, you will fall asleep in a state of mind, body and spirit coherence – you can't get much better sleep than that.

Why Bitches of A Feather Should Flock Together

When I look at the word community, I see two words: common-unity. I cannot stress the importance of surrounding ourselves with other women who share our beliefs, our concerns, our commitments in the world and who truly want us to win. The community you choose to identify with must offer a level playing field for all members. In other words, there is no one leader; there are no followers. Even better, everyone should have their unique gift that they bring to your community circle. This gift should be something that significantly contributes to you all.

Geese wonderfully exemplify the give and take dynamic responsible for creating powerful communities. I'm sure you have gazed at the morning or afternoon sky only to marvel at the geese flying in a perfect V-shaped formation. According to scientific studies, the geese fly in a V-shaped formation for two very empowering reasons. The first reason is, the geese understand the importance of not stressing out and conserving energy. Bringing their A game to V-formation, each bird intentionally flies slightly below the bird in front of them to reduce resistance from the wind and of course, conserve energy. The bird out front gives it all she's got and then when she's tired she falls to the back of the fleet, and the next bird takes the lead. This formulation allows the birds to fly farther as a community than they could if they were to fly solo.

The same holds true for us humans, there is power in unity, and when we women come together at the level of community, we have the power to move heaven and earth. Besides the results we can physically accomplish as a community, positive social interactions contribute significantly to our mental and physical health. There is nothing quite as soothing as a supportive arm wrapped around your shoulders when you are upset, assuring you, everything is going to be alright. As you will learn in the next chapter, certain types of touch instantly reduce heart rates, can suppress hysteria and eventually interrupt cortisol surges. By the way, the second reason geese fly in V formation is because it is the easiest way for each member to keep tabs on one another. So, I urge you, if you have not already done so, find your community of Responsible Bitches that can help you and that you can help and together, you continue to soar.

The last piece of advice I must offer you when it comes to participating in communities is that there are three kinds of women found in communities. There are women who are reputations, ~~and~~ there are women who are stereotypes and there are women that are specific archetypes – I will say more about that later. What I would like you to understand now is that a reputation is a persona you build on your merit and hard work. A stereotype is an image you borrow and merge with based on your affiliations. In other words, stereotypes are carbon copies of one another; they are typical. There is nothing typical about us Responsible Bitches. We are not screenshots of anyone. Responsible Bitches are reputations, re-presenting something special and unique to our communities. Another clear and defining difference between a stereotype and a reputation is that a stereotype woman is almost always looking to be compensated by her community. Reputations primarily look to contribute.

Spiritual Healing

As you may have gathered by now, I have an excellent collection of tools to help me maintain my Responsible Bitch disposition in life. However, bar none, the most significant tool I can ever grasp ahold of to regulate my emotions is my relationship to my spiritual practices. These practices include laughter, generosity, prayer and meditation. I believe the practice of spirituality should include those things that keep us in spirit and therefore, inspired. Inspired to be Responsible Bitches to be exact; responsible for replacing anger with laughter, selfishness with generosity, remorse with prayer and agitation with meditation.

I am not a big television person. However, my favorite source for laughter does come from watching the television show, America's Funniest Home Videos. I pre-record the episodes and I make it my business to watch at least one hour per week. I love silly humor and by the end of that one hour I find myself laughing so hard, my belly aches - in a good way, of course. Not only does laughter feel good, it is extremely healthy for us. Research confirms, laughter reduces cortisol levels while increasing the release of endorphins that leave us feeling fabulous long after the joke is over. Laughter has also been known to boost our immune systems, increase our resilience, cure depression and eliminate pain. I highly recommend, the next time you even think your bitch button is close to being pushed, force yourself to laugh. If that feels too weird, then try smiling really quick for a few seconds. The act of smiling stimulates the two facial muscles, the zygomatic major and the orbicularis oculi, that trigger the release of feel good endorphins.

Generosity is a fun spiritual practice and one that is perhaps the easiest to do. This particular practice is one that I almost immediately assign to my clients because it works well. The bottom line is, if there is something you really want, start giving that very thing away and it will come back to you. In other words, we must give the most what we want the most. If I have a client suffering from sadness and they sincerely want to find a way to be happy, I advise them to foster an abused dog and make it their business to bring profound joy into that dog's life every day. If I have a client who is depressed and just sick of life, I instruct her to find a dying plant. I then inform her that her only job is to find ways to bring that plant back to life. I am also a big fan of practicing random acts of love and kindness. This form of generosity often provides pleasure for both the giver and the receiver. Recent studies have shown, those who simply witness the act, experiences similar pleasure.

My spiritual practice of prayer and meditation are for the most part one in the same. To me, prayer is simply the practice of continuously giving thanks for everything, all day. As a result of my remaining in a constant state of gratitude, I find the universe is always providing me with more things to be grateful for. On the other hand, when I lived my life primarily as a reckless bitch, always whining about what I did not have, the universe made me right about that too. My meditation practice really helped me make the transition from reckless bitch to Responsible Bitch.

The type of meditation I practice is a silent mantra meditation introduced in the 1950's by yogi Maharishi Mahesh and it's called, Transcendental Meditation. I have been practicing this unique form of mindful meditation for nearly five years now, and it continues to provide me with the strength and guidance I need to live as a

Responsible Bitch. Much like my yoga practice, I consider meditation to be a spiritual practice that I depend on for my physical existence. It is through my meditation practice that I can communicate and interact with my creator by merely listening to my heart, tapping into my soul and tuning in to a higher level of intelligence. I do my best to meditate twice a day for twenty minutes each time. While sitting in meditation, I am often afforded the opportunity to address and transform toxic emotional issues such as anger from a spiritual perspective without much effort at all. This process is possible because when we sit in a calm, attuned state and offer our thoughts the quiet attention they desire, allowance replaces suppression. When there is no suppression, there is no resistance. When there is no resistance, there is no tension. The absence of tension and the presence of peace in our hearts and minds makes our bitch buttons and triggers that much harder to be charged.

Learning the practice of Transcendental Meditation might be a bit pricey for some. Although I highly recommend it for everyone on the planet, if you are not able to afford to learn how to do Transcendental Meditation right now, there is another way to derive the same if not similar value. I instruct my clients to set twenty minutes aside each day to think. Yes, I am suggesting that you do the same. Just find a comfortable and hopefully quiet place to sit and think for twenty minutes with your eyes gently closed. Traditionally we have been taught that meditation is the practice of sitting quiet and clearing your head and trying to think of nothing. What I love about the mindfulness approach is that you are encouraged to think about everything that is beckoning for your time and your mental attention.

When we surrender and make space for the thoughts that want to be known by us, we then satisfy their desire and they eventually do move on. It is only what we resist that will continue to persist. For example, if you are practicing what I refer to as old school meditation practices - when a thought comes up, you say to the thought, "go away. I can't think of you right now." Again, resistance causes persistence, so the thought remains, and your attempt to clear your mind fails. Instead of dealing with your feelings of failure, you fall asleep, and there goes your meditation session. Although falling asleep is not a bad thing during meditation, it's just not something you want to do as a result of feeling like a failure. By intentionally offering a space and a place for whatever thoughts want to come to you, you allow that thought to come to you and then once you think about it from every angle you simply place that thought on a cloud and imagine that thought being lifted up into the sky and floating off and away from you. The Mindfulness meditation practice is all about clearing the space and allowing what is there to be seen and then set free.

If you choose to take on this Mindful spiritual practice, I also suggest you use the tail end of your meditation practice to stock up on the vitality hormone, DHEA. By practicing five minutes of the Quick Coherence Technique twice a day, you will be able to stock up on twenty-four hours of DHEA every day. The immediate benefits I have noticed from this practice is that I don't jump at loud sounds anymore and when confronted with a challenge, stressor or threat, I find myself growing strangely calm instead of angry. This is what I meant when I told you, reading this book would equip you with the information needed in order to dodge that ol'cortisol bullet. My incident with Madam Gorgeousness the other day was the closest I have come to being triggered in months. Mind you; this is a vast departure from my past. Ask anyone who used to know me and you will hear things like, "she's a drama queen", or "she will cuss your ass out in a heartbeat," or "don't mess with Troy, she's a reckless bitch!" Ahhhh...it's lovely to have such a margin of personal testimonies to measure the distance I have traveled thus far. Okay, let's add another power tool to our Responsible Bitch belts, shall we?

Emotion Regulation Technique #2
Emotional Freedom Tapping (EFT)

Emotion Freedom Technique (EFT) is a technique that serves as a hybrid between psychology and Chinese acupressure. This self-administered therapy process entails using your fingers to tap on specific meridian points on your body. By tapping, you are using your natural energy to unlock and move energy through your body that has been stopped or stuck as we discussed earlier. Tapping has been scientifically proven to make measurable differences in your emotional and physical states. When practiced correctly, EFT can quickly reduce your immediate experience of anger or overwhelm. EFT is also a great technique to use during all stressful situations such as heated arguments or when re-telling a story that has an emotional charge. During an argument or stressful situation, EFT will keep your energy flowing, and as long as your energy is flowing, you will maintain a sense of ease in spite of the diseased space you may be in. EFT is also a terrific pain reducer that works well on migraines, menstrual cramps, menopause symptoms and other physical pains and challenges.

The 5 Steps of The EFT Tapping Process

1. Identify the Issue:

   For the sake of this lesson, we will use anger as the issue you are tapping on. Please note, you can tap on as many things as you like but you must only tap on one issue at a time.

2. Determine Your Level Of Anger:

   Assign your current anger a level of intensity on a scale from 0-10. This will be the margin we use to monitor your progress after you complete each tapping round.

3. The Activation:

The activation process wakes your energy system up, informing it that you are ready to work with it. The activation process happens when you use the tips of the fingers on your left hand to tap on the Karate Chop (KC) side of your right hand.

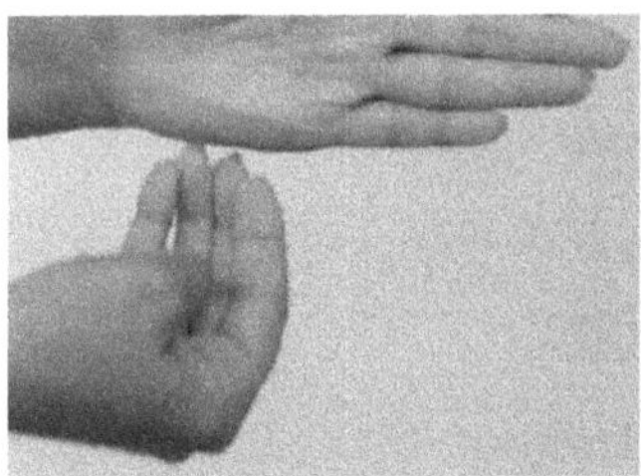

As

you tap on the (KC) point, you will simultaneously say….

"Even though I have this anger, I deeply and completely accept myself."

Please repeat the above sentence two or three times and make sure you are powerfully present to your anger while doing so. Do not try to repress the emotion, if anything you want it at its peak during this first step.

4. Tapping On the Other Points

Once you have activated your energy system by tapping on your (KC) point, for at least ten seconds, you can move on. Using the tips of your two right fingers, tap on each of the points in the order as listed below. As you tap on the next seven points for five seconds each, you will simultaneously and repeatedly say: "Even though…."

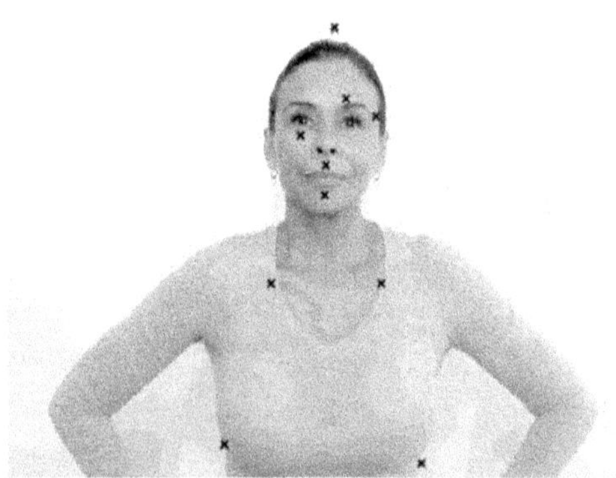

Beginning of the Eyebrow (EB)

Side of the Eye (SE)

Under the Eye (UE)

Under the Nose (UN)

Chin Point (CH)

Beneath the Collarbone (CB)

Under the Arm (UA)

Top of the Head (TOH)

5. Test Level of Anger

Lowering your hand from your last tapping point (TOH) inhale and exhale deeply. Check in with the intensity level of your anger and then assign your current anger a level of intensity on a scale from 0-10. If there is there has not been 90% improvement, please prepare to tap another round, using the same process. Depending on the intensity of your anger, you may need to do several rounds.

Congratulations! You now know another powerful emotion regulation technique that promises to help you keep your Responsible Bitch disposition alive.

CHAPTER 5
YOU BY DESIGN

Context Is Everything

What makes context so powerful is the fact that the context is always decisive. Once you know the context of something, you can accurately predict the content of that very thing. Take for instance if you have a book, and the title of the book is, "How to Make Cookies" the content is certain to be instructional advice on making cookies. Again, when you know the context, you can pretty much, predict the content. The same holds true for all areas of life. I often use this practice when I am interviewing new clients. Once I understand the context of their life, I pretty much know their whole story. Unfortunately, many people are not aware of this very important fact and that is, if we do not consciously create a context for our lives, by default, a context will be assigned to us. Even worse, more often than not, the context that is assigned to us has everything to do with our triggers.

Assuming you are committed to living your life as a Responsibly Powerful Bitch, learning how to create an empowering context for yourself and understanding the context of others is non-negotiable. Reckless bitches have no regard for context because reckless bitches secretly want to remain victims. Victims live their lives moaning and groaning about all the bad things that have been done to them. The following perfectly illustrates a woman whose context was her trigger and the content of her life was consistent with her trigger. As a result, she lived her life every day as a depressed victim.

Help Me; Don't Help Me, Scenario #8

Hannah's trigger was born the day her uncle tied her to a tree in her backyard and left her there for hours. She was eight years old at the time. Hannah says, she screamed for help, but no one came to help her. She even remembers a school bus driving by and is certain the driver of the bus, and the kids saw her, but still did not stop to help her. Eventually, Hannah figured out a way to wiggle her tiny frame free from the ropes that held her to the tree. From that day, Hannah also decided she would never ask anyone to help her again. She also decided, because no one came to help her, she would never help anyone ever again. So, not only is Hannah's trigger, "no one will ever help me," it also became the context of her life. If the title of Hannah's book of life is called, "No One Will Ever Help Me" then that is also the context that she has been living her life inside of. Because the context decides the content, it is safe to say that the content of Hannah's life is filled with many occasions in which she voices a need for help but help never appears.

After learning of Hannah's context for life, she confirmed that she could ask five different people at work to help her with one simple task and without fail, all five would not be available to help her or ignore her request entirely. Hannah also sadly admitted, this is simply a reality she has learned to live with. When I explained to Hannah, this was only a reality because it is the context assigned to her life and context decides the content, she refused to believe me. When I then offered to help her create a new context, she instantly refused my help. I expected nothing less because contexts are double-edged swords. Hannah is certain no one will ever respond to her requests for help. As a self-protection mechanism, Hannah refuses to let anyone volunteer to help her nor will she volunteer to help anyone else. Hannah confirmed again, when someone wants or needs her help, it pisses her off. She is then instantly triggered because she is already convinced, if she needed help, they would not help her. So, when I offered to help Hannah, she became triggered because she did not believe I could help her. She also did not want to set herself up to be indebted to me for trying.

Hannah's scenario is the trap that we accidentally fall into, and then after decades of failed attempts to break free from this trap, we become bitter and angry. We accept these shitty contexts as our lives. However, the great news is that as Responsibly Powerful Bitches, we can create whatever context for our lives that we want. We just have to take time to consciously create it. Remember, if we do not consciously choose and create a context for ourselves, by default, our triggers or other influences will create our context for us. This happens because we cannot just wander through life without a context. Everyone and for the most part, everything has a context. The other thing about having a disempowering context like Hannah is that we spend our entire lives attracting people and situations into our lives to make us right about our contexts. In other words, we become context confirmation magnets, attracting all things in the universe to make us right about what we believe our context to be. In Hannah's case, her confirmation magnet continually created instances where she was forced to ask for help only to be disappointed by the response. Or, again, the flip side is, people who she believed would never help her would have the audacity to ask her for help. At this point, I hope that you are biting at the bit, anxious to determine your context and create a new one if the one you currently have been living with is your trigger or disempowering in any way. So, let's take a look, shall we?

The best way to determine your context is to look at the trigger you distinguished for yourself in Chapter 3 and decide if your life experiences seem to revolve around that particular trigger. For example, if your trigger is rejection, look to see if you spend the majority of your time working your ass off to avoid rejection or do you find yourself constantly rejecting people, places, and things? As I mentioned earlier, once our contexts are assigned, we subconsciously and often consciously become confirmation magnets, always looking to be right about the context we believe ourselves to be. That being so, wouldn't it be great to create a context that felt great to be right about? Instead of attracting experiences that make you right about the fact that people don't help you or you're always being abandoned, how about confirming a context that makes you feel fabulous about yourself?

Pay Attention to Your Intentions

Before I guide you through the steps necessary to responsibly create a new and empowering context for yourself, it is important that you truly understand what you are up to in life and that you at least have an idea about what you want to be up to in life. Please note that most of us could drive a freight train through the gap that exists between what we want to be up to in life and what we are actually up to in life. The quickest way I know to personally bridge this gap is to pay attention to our intentions. It is not simply enough to want something. Granted, knowing what you want is a great place to start. However, on the heels of being clear on what it is that you want, you must become highly intentional about it. It should not come as any surprise to learn that your intention will be very instrumental in the creation of your new context because where your intention goes, your attention flows. And, what we focus on the most is what we become magnets for. The other thing that is so great about setting your intention is that when you do, it leaves little to no room for nonsense or reckless bitch behavior. When and if reckless bitch behavior does attempt to show its ugly head, it bumps up so hard against your intentions that it stands out like a sore thumb.

The other important thing about intention is that it is a spiritual GPS. Based on your connection to your intentions, you will be firmly pointed in the direction you want to go. Additionally, the more intentional you can be then the more you create a vibrational frequency for that which you want to attract in your life. Intentions are also good preservers of time because when we are intentional, it is harder to waste time. Time management continues to be a challenge in my life. It is because of this challenge that I rarely take on any task unless I am one-hundred percent clear of my intention. When I refer to a task, I am including everything that involves my participation from volunteering at my son's school to hosting a dinner party to watching a movie. I always set an intention with the outcome I want in mind. Now, I am not saying I am 100% attached to all of my intentions, however, starting out with an intention allows me to create a possible future for myself as it pertains to the task. It gives me the opportunity to be in charge of my life and responsible for my life experiences. This Responsibly Powerful Bitch tactic keeps my game tight and right.

Here is a quasi-superficial example of the power of intention but one that might hit home. Let's pretend, your husband, who also happens to be the man of your dreams, informs you, he wants to take you to Bora Bora in two months for a two-week vacation. He goes on to tell you, while in Bora Bora, he has one wish. His wish is to see you running around all day in the beautiful designer swimsuits that he wants you to pick out and that he will pay for. Fast forward a few hours later, that night, you go out to dinner with your girlfriends, and you tell them the exciting news about your future vacation. You share your husband's one wish with your friends, and in spite of the extra weight you have been carrying around since the birth of your twenty-year-old son, you have every intention of making his dream come true. Your friends applaud your commitment. Dinner is over, and the dessert tray is presented by the waiter. Question. How many pieces of cheesecake are you going to eat for dessert? Zero, right? Why? Because you have every intention of looking fabulous in those swimsuits while vacationing in Bora Bora. That intention will not only point you in the right direction; it will keep you inspired along the way. Bottom line; Intentions are vibrational frequencies that help us to keep our eye on the prize until our commitments are fulfilled.

What Are Your Committed To?

If intention is the bridge that closes the gap between what we want to be up to in life and what we are really up to in life, the only thing left to do is decide what we want to be up to in life. And, even more important is to examine our commitment to what we say we want to be up to.

"If you want to know what you are committed to, look at what you've got." -Werner Erhardt

For most of my adult life, I pretended that what I was up to was making a name for myself in the entertainment industry as an actress, writer, and film director. I can now call bullshit on myself and confirm that this was a huge pretense because what I really was up to in life was not that. I despised acting classes, I took one screen writing course in the fifteen years I called myself a screenwriter, and unlike most serious directors, I had no interest in studying the great filmmakers of the past. I hated reading screenplays and I rarely even went to the movies. I simply was not committed to what I was saying I was up to. I was not committed because I was not inspired. To be inspired is to be in-spirit. To be in spirit is to commit to the fulfillment of a desire that comes from your heart. A career in show business was not a desire that came from my heart. A career in show business was a desire that came from my head. As I mentioned earlier, for all practical and logical reasons, it made sense, and it was a hell of a lot better than just being someone's secretary. If I ever make a commitment to act, write a screenplay or direct again, I will only do so because it is a desire of my heart and because I am authentically inspired to do so.

If you are now wondering what you are committed to, really committed to, simply look at what you have got. If you are in a shitty relationship, it is because, on some level, that is what you are committed to. If you are in a great relationship, it is because, on some level, that is what you are committed to. I assert, what we want to be up to is that which we are committed to. So, the real question on the table here is, what do you want to responsibly be committed to? This question is so powerful because it is the question that will support you with the creation of your next context. The following scenario is a wonderful example of a woman who un-collapsed what she said she was up to and what she really wanted to be committed to.

Giving Up the Green, To Go Green, Scenario #8

I have a close friend who I will refer to as Melissa. Melissa was once a very successful divorce attorney. She worked for one of the largest law firms in Beverly Hills. She also litigated some of the most famous divorces in history. Without a doubt, Melissa was on track to make a partner at the prestigious firm before the age of forty. However, after her first child was born with a challenging respiratory issue, Melissa's commitments changed. She no longer wanted to be committed to her lucrative and prestigious career as a hot-shot attorney. Her new context as a nurturing mother altered her intentions in life and she wanted to commit to finding a cure for her son's health challenge. Inside of her new context, armed with powerful intentions, she fulfilled on her commitment to discovering her son was allergic to a toxic ingredient used in the supposedly non-allergenic laundry soap for sensitive babies. No stranger to balancing the scales of justice, Melissa took the legal steps necessary to force proper labeling on the falsely advertised product. Not stopping there, Melissa went on to create one of the largest sustainable lifestyle on-line green stores, specializing in natural, organic and ethically sourced products. In addition to offering superb, eco-friendly products to people around the world, Melissa is perfectly poised to one day sell her company for millions of dollars if she should so choose to do so.

I am a strong believer our pain can lead us directly to our purpose. Melissa could not tolerate seeing her child suffer. Like most nurturing mothers, our child's pain is our pain. That being so, Melissa moved toward her pain and that movement eventually led her to what has now become her life purpose. My story is quite similar. My pain was a direct result of my anger issues. Moving towards my anger and my desire to help other women in my position, I found my life purpose. So, if you have not found your life purpose yet, or if you are not sure if you are pursuing your life purpose and therefore you are not sure what you want to commit yourself to, this next exercise will provide you with an inspiring dose of insight. If you have found your purpose and you are sure what you want to commit to in life then, high five, sister! However, the following exercise will also be beneficial for you because it might do one of two things. It might confirm you are on the right road; it might show you an additional path you can attach to the road you are on, or both.

You By Design Exercise

Please answer the following questions as authentically as you possibly can.

1. I have so much fun and lose all track of time when I am doing the following activity: *(Troy: when I am teaching people how to intercept their negative emotions)*

2. The positive emotion that I feel would best compliment this activity would be: *(Troy: happiness)*

3. If I were to combine this activity and this emotion, I

would have the following two words: *(Troy: teaching happiness)*

4. If I were to create a new context for myself out of the activity and the emotion chosen above, the context would be: *(Troy: Teacher of Happiness)*

5. If I were to create my life inside of this new context, my intention would be to (Troy: to learn as much as I can on the subject and travel the world teaching people how to dissolve all barriers that stand between them and their happiness)

6. The final step in the creation process is to then declare with absolute certainty that which you have created. *(Troy: I am a teacher of happiness)*

As you may have gathered from these questions, the most important thing we can do for ourselves is to pursue a career that revolves around an activity that we lose ourselves to. When we take that activity and then attach it to an emotion that compliments the task and or inspires us, we are designing a new context. This new context is being created from a space of being in-spirit or from our hearts instead of our heads. We can then confirm the new context is the perfect choice for us by examining the intention that context inspires in us. If you can powerfully connect to the intention as something you would want to commit yourself to fulfilling then a celebration is in order. Your new context has been discovered.

Discovering your new context is wonderful, but I want to pause long enough to underscore the importance of number 6, the final step. Remember, by default; you have a context that has been creating the reality of your life for you. To dismiss this old context and replace it with the new context, a declaration in language must be made with a force of passion. All things are created in language. This goes as far back as the Old Testament when God said, "let there be light." God did not think there should be light. Again, the Bible reads, God, said, "let there be light.' In the same way that God created light with language, you will create your new context with the use of language. This new context creation is as simple as your declaring, I AM (insert new context here).

Unless you have serious magical powers, your new context

will not instantly become your current reality. For most of us it takes at least a couple of days before we become a vibrational frequency match for our new context. It is then that the universe will begin to conspire on your behalf, drawing that reality to you with magnetic forces, because it is you. However, remember, it works both ways. If you create a negative context, you will still be a context confirmation magnet, attracting to you that which you contextually are. The universe does not care if you are your context by default or creation. The universe simply loves to obey its own law and that is to play matchmaker, bringing things that share a likeness together.

Granted, when our default contexts were created years ago, we did not intentionally speak such nonsense into existence. However, because most contexts created by default are triggers, somewhere along our journey, we did make declarations consistent with the default way of being, thus activating the law of attraction. For example, when Hannah finally freed herself from the tree, she declared something along the lines, people will never help me and because of that, I will never help people. She got to be one-hundred percent right about her reality because her life existed within the context she used language to create it with.

Our words are our wands. Once we know what we want, our language will bring it into existence because language represents thought, thought represents feelings and feelings become things. It holds true, once we decide what we do not want, language will free us from it. I must warn you, removing things with language must be worded slightly different. What I have come to realize is the universe does not pay attention to the words "don't" or "want" so if you say, I don't want to be fat. The universe hears, "I to be fat." At that point, it gets to work, eagerly providing you with all the temptation you need to be fat. A better declaration to handle a weight issue would be the following language: "I choose to be thin" or "I am thin". I say all this to explain to you why, if I were to say, "I want to be a teacher of happiness" the universe would ignore the word *want* and hear, "I to be a teacher of happiness." As a result, I would never actually be a teacher of happiness, and it would remain something I am to be, one day someday. So, I would be left wanting that experience instead of having it. This is why I am urging you to speak your context into existence by declaring it as I did mine. My declaration was, "I am a teacher of happiness." Lastly, unless we want to insult the universe's intelligence, we must declare what we are as a context once and then give thanks or express gratitude every second we can after that. Here's an example:

> Declaration: I am a teacher of happiness.
>
> Expression of Gratitude: I give thanks that I am a happiness teacher every day and in every way.

CHAPTER 6
THE POWER OF BEING PISSED

Guiding Your Anger

Anger is a very interesting emotion. There are many roads that can lead us to anger, but once we arrive at that destination, the reality of anger seems to have a universal tonality to it. Granted, some expressions of anger are stronger than others. And yes, for some others, anger is the precursor to rage. However, for the most part, anger is a force of energy that seems to show up when all other forces have failed. Why does it show up? Most often because there is a threat and there is something that anger wants to protect. The protection sought after is often an intense desire for the long-overdue realization of a specific result. Once that result is produced, for the most part, anger shifts towards a decline. If the desired result is not produced, anger is renowned for its intensity and ability to expand with the fervor of a fierce runaway fire.

Most Responsible Bitches fear their anger and rightfully so. Most reckless bitches deny or resist their anger which is why their anger has a hairline trigger - remember what we resist will persist. Others attempt to dominate their anger which amounts to anger trying to tame anger. Some turn their anger inward; de-pressing their anger, guess what we call that? If depression is not your style then perhaps you become a full-blown screamer or shouter, both of which are potential precursors for heart attacks. Some of us choose to pop pills to remain chill, and some of us choose to self-medicate - a lot. Honestly, however you choose to deal with your anger is well, quite frankly, between you and your anger. However, I firmly believe, when we face what we fear, when we face what is chasing, annoying or eating at us, something even more powerful appears.

What could be more powerful than fear? How about having faith in our anger, believing it is present to help us push through emotions or experiences that may be energetically stopped or stuck in or around us. What if we could use the onset of our anger as a mere wake-up call, alerting us that it is time to get serious while remaining clear? I'm not suggesting we not allow ourselves to experience anger. To the contrary, I am urging you to experience your anger but just in a safer environment. The environment I am referring to is your heart space instead of your head. This shift from head to heart is the difference between us being reckless bitches and Responsible Bitches. The deciding factor is, scientifically proven, to be nothing more than choosing where we want to breathe from. The fact of the matter is we have to breathe anyway, so why not breathe from an empowering space when your power is threatened as opposed to doing the opposite. If it is just a matter of making a simple conscious decision to drop out of your head and into your heart's intelligence to avoid a cortisol surge while obtaining information on how to proceed, why wouldn't you? Even still, as an angered person, your next course of action may require screaming or a bit of angry seething. This process does not numb you down; it simply smartens you up. Then, from your heart space, you can express anger without fear. You can make demands for results without hostility. You can resume your composure without the lingering cortisol that would have otherwise been created.

If you think I am asking you to be one-hundred percent responsible for the intelligence that manages your anger, you are one hundred percent correct. If you think I am asking you to do anything this former reckless bitch, now uber Responsible Bitch has not done, you are one hundred percent incorrect. I learned years ago; my leadership has nothing to do with the number of followers I have. I am a leader, in my mind, simply because when it comes to leading, I am willing to always go first. Period. End of story and that is the story I am forever sticking to. So, okay. You may be wondering if it is really possible for you to express your anger while activating your heart's intelligence and speaking your piece from that environment as opposed to your head. I can assure you there is only one way for you to find out. I am not urging you to get pissed off, but I am suggesting you get a bit annoyed. I am sure you can find something to get annoyed about in the next few minutes. My suggestion, scan your wall on Facebook page, something is bound to snag you. Before implementing your emotion regulation test-drive, be sure to have the Quick Coherence heart breathing technique steps in front of you. You will find them at the end of chapter three. Once you are present to annoyance, simply move through the steps and watch how quickly your annoyance will disappear.

NOTE: It is worth mentioning again and again if you choose to manage your anger from your head's intelligence, once your anger triggers a certain amount of the stress hormone cortisol into your system, you will be emotionally hijacked by the reptilian brain and what you do after that is anybody's guess.

However, if you can remember to drop into your heart's intelligence by simply breathing five seconds in, eight seconds out, you stand a loving chance at expressing your anger in a healthy way and avoiding the negative influences and consequences of your reptilian brain.

Know Your Space & Place

It is my deepest desire that you master the privilege it is to express anger through your heart's intelligence as opposed to your head's intelligence. However, even more importantly, if is my most profound prayer that all my sisters understand, there is a time and place for everything - yes, that especially includes your responsible expressions of anger. Part of our responsibility includes knowing when to go off, where to go off and when to hold off. It all depends on the result we are committed to creating with our anger. If we want to produce a positive result from a potentially negative situation, we have to make sure we address the situation inside of a condition that is conducive to that success. Just think of a petri dish used to grow certain kinds of bacteria. To grow the bacteria, there has to be a condition (space and place) that is a match for the bacteria you want to grow. So if you are upset and having a heated discussion with someone, the responsible thing to do is to make sure that the space and the place provide the correct condition needed to produce the results that you want from that argument. For example, if you're arguing with your spouse at the grocery store, chances are a grocery store environment will not offer you the condition needed to reach a peaceful resolution. However, if you have a disagreement with your spouse and decide to address it further in the privacy of your home, you are responsibly awaiting a condition conducive with the possibility of a successful resolution.

It goes without saying, reckless bitches can care less about the space, place, arguing from their hearts or finding the best physical condition to resolve their upsets. Once they are upset, they have little to no regard for what they say or who they say it to. True to their namesake, they become reckless. Mind you, even the sanest women can become reckless, if and when their reptilian brain takes over. The following scenario is a very unfortunate scenario of a well-educated, typically responsible woman who was hijacked by a cortisol surge that later activated her reptilian brain.

She Didn't Have To Die, Scenario #9

A twenty-eight year old woman is pulled over by a police officer for a minor traffic violation. The officer gathers the necessary paperwork from the female driver and returns minutes later. As he hands her back her paperwork:

Officer: Okay. Ma'am, you okay?
Woman: I'm waiting on you, this is your job.
Officer: I don't know, you seem very irritated.
Woman: I am, I really am.

The woman then continues to complain about being pulled over and reprimands the officer for giving her a warning ticket for the minor traffic violation. Continuing on her tyrant, the officer then asks:

Officer: Are you done?"
Woman: You asked what was wrong and I told you. So, now I'm done, yeah.
Officer: Okay.

Puffing on her lit cigarette, the woman then exhales a generous amount of smoke. The officer is less than pleased by the gesture.

Officer: You mind putting out your cigarette, please?
Woman: I'm in my car, why do I have to put out my cigarette?

Irritated by her response, the officer then demands—

Officer: Oh, you can step on out now.
Woman: I don't have to step out of my car.

Officer: Step out of the car.

The officer opens her car door, firmly demanding her to step out of the car. The woman firmly informs the officer, he does not have the right to demand her to step of the car.

Officer: I do have the right, now step out or I will remove you.

Woman: I refuse to talk to you other than to identify myself…

Officer: Step out...or I will remove you.

Woman: I am getting removed for a failure to signal?

Officer: Step out, or I will remove you. I'm giving you a lawful order. Get out of the car now, or I am going to remove you.

Woman: I'm calling my lawyer.

Officer: I'm going to yank you out of here.

Woman: You're going to yank me out of my car? Ok, alright. Let's do this.

The officer reaches into the car and grabs her.

Officer: We are going to!

Woman: Don't touch me!

Officer: Get out of the car!

Woman: Don't touch me! I'm not under arrest! You

don't have the right to yank me out of the car!

Officer: You are under arrest!

Woman: I'm under arrest, for what?! For what?! Why am I being apprehended?!

The officer then removes his gun, aims it at her and demands that the woman get out of the car. She immediately gets out of the car and heads for the curb. He follows her with his pistol aimed at her.

Woman: Wow, all this for a failure to signal?! Right, yea! Let's take this to court!

She removes her cell phone and attempts to record the incident. The officer demands she put the phone away. As he struggles to put handcuffs on her—

Woman: You feel good about yourself, don't you?! Why am I being arrested?! Are you fucking kidding me?! And you're full of shit. Fucking scared of a female.

The woman proceeds to call the officer the most derogatory names she could think of. The officer continued to physically dominate her into submission. Eventually, the woman was handcuffed and placed into the back of the patrol car and taken to jail. Three days later, she was found dead in her jail cell. Allegedly, she hung herself. When I first learned of this story, I was devastated because this is a clear and concise example of how both parties could have done better if only they knew better.

Let's review the first part of the situation and point out the different choices available that would have produced different results. Different results that could have prevented the arrest that led to the jail cell death.

Officer: Okay. Ma'am, you okay?

Woman: I'm waiting on you, this is your job.

Officer: I don't know, you seem very irritated.

Woman: I am, I really am.

Red Flag for The Woman:

At this point, the woman's heart rate is elevated, and the threat of damage has most likely already activated her cortisol.

Solution for The Woman:

Heart focus breathing, five seconds in, eight seconds out would instantly shift her into her heart's intelligence, calming her down.

She continues to complain.

Officer: Are you done?"

Woman: You asked what was wrong and I told you. So, now I'm done, yeah.

Officer: Okay.

Puffing on her lit cigarette, the woman then exhales a generous amount of smoke. The officer is less than pleased by the gesture.

Officer: You mind putting out your cigarette, please?

Woman: I'm in my car, why do I have to put out my cigarette?

Red Flag for The Officer:

At this point, the officer's heart rate is increasing due to the health threat the woman's second-hand smoke poses for him. He has clearly been triggered by her refusal to put her cigarette out. Him being triggered is indicative of him then instructing her to step out of the car. The officer's trigger is most likely along the lines of "people don't care about me".

Solution for The Officer:

If the officer was consciously aware of his trigger, he could have implemented an emotion regulation technique such as tapping or heart-focused breathing to keep his temper in check and interrupt his cortisol surge.

Red Flag for The Woman:

Committing an annoying act such as exhaling a mouth full of smoke near the face of someone who has the upper hand is realistically just not a favorable condition to put ourselves in. Yes, the woman had the right to smoke in her car. However, we must be aware of the consequences associated with certain conditions before attempting to put our foot down and demand justice prevail. I am not saying it is right; I am just keeping it real. On every level, the woman was the inferior of the two. If we are going to take a stand for ourselves, we must be sure there is a solid ground beneath us. This comes from being aware of our space, place and necessary conditions to at least have a shot at winning.

Solution for The Woman:

By authentically acknowledging the reality of her condition, the woman would have realized that she was not in a space or place to exert power. Again, I am not saying it is right. Truthfully, I am the first to admit; there are many holes in our legal and judicial system. Having to surrender and experience ourselves as powerless in a situation is never easy. However, had the woman accepted that the condition needed for justice to prevail was temporarily not available she might have made life-altering decisions. She might have put her cigarette out, signed the warning ticket and later filed a complaint against the officer to her heart's content.

To this day, the story of this woman's death breaks my heart. Her story was one of several stories that inspired me to write this book. In addition to the enormous amount of stress the altercation and the arrest had on her nervous system, she sat in jail for three days before her death. I can only imagine how saturated her system must have been with cortisol prior to her allegedly taking her own life. The bottom line is, had she understood the importance of space and place, she might have still been alive today.

The Importance of Creativity

Most of the women I have had the privilege to work with all seem to have one thing in common; they have no idea what their purpose in life is. Not to undermine wife-life and motherhood, but many of the women who are wives or mothers, also long to find a form of expression that represents who they are for themselves. For many years, I led a program designed to support people in finding their self-expression in the world. I would then coach them in such a way that they would create a project that carries the essence of their self-expression and then have that project make a difference for an underserved community.

For example, one participant decided her self-expression had to do with freedom and joy. The underserved community that she wanted to make a difference for was the blind community. With her self-expression of freedom and joy in mind, she organized a ballroom dance for the blind community and called it, "Dancing In The Dark." She and her team put eucalyptus oil on the pillars, doors, and walls to steer the blind dancers away from potential danger. She and her team then gave the dancers lavender oil to wear on their bodies to help manage the distance between them and other dancers while dancing.

The event was a smash hit that has since become an annual event. Without a doubt, the creation and organization of this event is this woman's self-expression in the world. The event allows her to be fully present to her life purpose which is to create joy and freedom for others and in turn, she gets to experience joy and freedom.

Not knowing our purpose in the world can be a very frustrating experience. More often than not, the purpose the women I work with are seeking has to do with unleashing their creativity. It's worth stating again, in life we humans are almost always doing two things, we are either creating or surviving. Even more specific, I have found that those who are surviving are also living on the reckless bitch side of life because, for the most part, their desperation for survival also has them grasping anxiously at straws.

So, what's an angry woman stuck in survival to do? Dance. Seriously, if you find that you are in a constant state of survival and almost always angry as a result of it, dance. My plant medicine Shaman, Mitra Reuven Politi believes the act of dancing is a sure and fast way to move the stuck and stopped energy that leads to anger. Mitra explained, the reason dancing is such a powerful anecdote for anger is that it is a creative process and most anger is masking a spiritual experience of creative frustration. He also believes dancing can help to generate the two emotions necessary to heal anger organically. These two emotions are forgiveness and acceptance. Granted, after removing your experience of anger by dancing, the need for surviving daily stressors, threats and challenges may still be present. However, it is much easier to create a plan to transform these stressors, threats and challenges when you are not continuously being confronted with anger.

Worthy Opponents

I am always very particular as to whom I choose to argue with. Quite frankly, no one is worth my having a cortisol surge. However, unless we live in a glass bubble, upsets are inevitable because they are the direct result of expectations being unfulfilled. I learned a long time ago, if I wanted to manage the drama in my life, I would have to learn to manage my expectations, more specifically, I had to manage who I expected things from. I stopped expecting things from people who had a history of disappointing me.

No expectation, no upset. It really is that simple. If you do not give a person the ammunition to shoot you down, you won't get shot down. That being said, chances are, there will always be at least one person you do have expectations of. Chances are also good, this person will have expectations of you. Again, expectations unfulfilled are the primary causes of upset. I call these individuals my worthy opponents. These are individuals that I feel it is worth stepping into the ring and going a few rounds with to resolve whatever issues may come up. But these are the only people I am ever willing to get all hot and bothered over. I am willing to go the distance with them because I know these individuals care about me and in the same way that they are my worthy opponent, I am the worthy opponent for them. As a result, we are always committed to one thing, no matter what and that is restoring the affinity between us after we have moved through the upset. The other thing that really works for me these days is like me; my worthy opponents agree to argue with me from their hearts. Arguments that used to last hours and spill into cortisol drenched days are over within minutes. It's an amazingly beautiful experience!

The Super Model & Me, Scenario #10

During the height of my career as an actress in the late 80s, I became best friends with a supermodel who has since earned quite a reputation for being a reckless bitch with serious anger issues. However at that time she was nowhere as bad as she became and I really enjoyed hanging out with her. We had a lot of fun together. For a while we were inseparable. At the time she was also dating one of the most famous actors in Hollywood. He was a guy who had once pursued me relentlessly but I never gave in to his advances because of the twenty-two year age difference. Although my super model friend was younger than me, she seemed to like being with an older man so, I was like, more power to you. The problem here was when he realized that she and I were such good friends he begged me not to tell her that he had ever pursued me. Granted, he and I were never lovers but still, he did not want her to know that he had been pining for the poonanny. No problem. I never said anything.

One day, my drama queen ex-bff suspected that her movie star boyfriend might have been cheating on her in his apartment. As her activated reptilian brain pondered ways to interrupt his rendezvous, she decided to call 911 and report a fire. She gave the emergency operator his address. I am sure you can imagine what happened next. He immediately suspected she had done it and she blamed it on me. Not only did she blame it on me, but she also begged me to accept blame if and when he confronted me. I reluctantly agreed to take the rap for her because I really could care less if he liked me or not and I wanted her to be with him again because she was truly in love with him.

Well, that was the beginning of the end of our friendship. After taking the wrap for her, I guess she was afraid that one day I might tell him the truth when confronted, so she started distancing herself from me. Then, just to make sure I was never able to get into that A-List click again she started bad-mouthing me and told all sorts of lies about me to all the people we knew, some of which I introduced her too. In actuality, she blackballed me. At the time, I did not even think to question the story she would have to fabricate for her to convince her movie star boyfriend that I made that 911 call. It had to be a hell of a story because when I ran into him years later, he cornered me and told me I was a very dangerous and evil person. He then stormed off before I could utter a single word.

In retrospect, it was interesting to see how one person could turn so many people against me. As sad as that experience was for me, I simply walked away. I thought of confronting her but the last time we had an altercation in which she attacked me in the street, it made headline news, and I just did not want that kind of press surrounding me. My reputation meant way more to me than adding my name to the list of women she has publicly attacked. She was not worth stepping into the ring for. Anyone who would want to hurt me so deeply to cover their tracks and a boldfaced lie could never be my worthy opponent. And all the people she took with her, should have gone with her because if they could walk away from me that fast, they were not my worthy opponents either.

> "Run from people who love drama, or they will put you in one of their episodes."
>
> -- Instagram Meme (author unknown)

When Your Partner Cheats

My perspective of infidelity is quite paradoxical in nature because, in the same way, I believe infidelity is the strongest form of betrayal, I believe betrayal is the number one cause of infidelity. My theory is somewhat confirmed by the fact that 99.9% of the women in the anger management program that I teach attribute their domestic violence to their unbearable feelings of betrayal. Below is a letter that was sent to my YouTube advice channel, called Troy Talks™. I am choosing to use this particular case to address infidelity because of the pristine clarity in the situation.

Help! My Wife Cheated On Me, Scenario #12

Dear Troy,

I just learned that my wife of 4 years has been having an affair with her boss. I am devastated and don't know what to do. My wife has expressed a great deal of remorse and regret and promised me that she won't cheat again. I don't know if I can trust her and open my heart to her again. My wife's job requires a lot of traveling and unfortunately her boss, the man she cheated on me with, often travels with her. My friends think I should leave her, but I want to believe that this was just a one-time mistake. Should I leave her? Should I trust her again? How will I know that she would never cheat on me again, especially when I know she will be traveling in the future with the same man. Can you please help me transform this now?

Lost & Confused, Robert

Dear Robert:

Thank you for writing in. My first question to you my friend is how are you cheating on yourself? I ask you this because if you see something in your life, somewhere, you are being that something in your life. In this case, you see cheating. So, I will ask you again, where in your life are you cheating on yourself? Life is always an inside job, so your wife cheating on you is nothing more than a physical manifestation of a personal internal experience that you are having with yourself. So, if you want to see something different out there in the world then something different needs to transform there inside of you.

Please know I am not trying to let your wife off the hook here. What I am committed to doing is keeping you from being anyone's victim. We go about avoiding the victim posture in life by looking to see how we can be responsible for that which is showing up in our world. Let me just break this down for you from a physics perspective. According to physics, no two things can exist in the same space at the same time. I will give you an example, hot is one thing, and cold is one thing. Hot and cold cannot exist in the same space at the same time. Loyalty and infidelity cannot exist in the same space at the same time. Again, if you see cheating in your life, it is because somewhere in your life, you are a cheater.

Now I know this advice sounds harsh and given what you are up against it's probably not what you want to hear, and it probably hit you right between the eyebrows. However, I want to keep it real with you. I could give you the sort of advice that would have you make your wife quit her job. I could also give you advice that would have you just run around trying to alter all sorts of circumstances that you truly, at the end of the day, have no control of including removing all temptation from your wife's path. That would do two things; one it would make you physically and emotionally exhausted. Two; in the long-term, it's not going to produce the results you're committed to producing. So, what there really is to do here, Robert is to look inside yourself. Look and see where have you been cheating on yourself? The bottom line is we teach people how to treat us. So, somewhere along the line, somewhere along the journey with your wife, by way of example, you taught her that it was okay for her to cheat on you. Now when she witnessed this maybe she lost respect for you, maybe she lost respect for your relationship, or maybe she just decided that you were not who she believed you to be after all.

Before you start beating yourself up and making yourself bad and wrong for who you weren't in that relationship, I want you to understand; there are no accidents. This is happening right now because now is the time for you to transform this experience of cheating in your life forever. Now is the time for you to take some personal inventory and look and see where have you given up on yourself. Maybe you have given up on one of your dreams. Maybe you are not managing your health and well-being the way you promised yourself that you would. Maybe there's some promise that you made to yourself a long time ago that you're just not fulfilling on. Somewhere there's a commitment that you made to yourself that you are not fulfilling on and how that shows up in the world is that people are not fulfilling the commitments that they made to you. So, what there is for you to do is really simple, and the great news is that if you take this advice, you will be at the source of your own transformation instead of the mercy of circumstances outside of you.

What there really is to do is just sit down, take some personal inventory, make a list, see where you gave up on yourself, see where you sold out on yourself, see what commitments you broke with yourself. When you do this, you will then restore the honor and loyalty into the relationship with yourself and 1 of 2 things will happen. The first thing that might happen is, your wife will notice a shift in the relationship that you are having with yourself, and she will start treating you with the same level of loyalty and honor that you are treating yourself with. The second thing that is possible is that once you start bringing that kind of loyalty and honor to yourself your wife may not be available to treat you the way that you're treating yourself. As a result; through grace and in perfect she will disappear completely from your life. She will disappear because she won't be a vibrational match for who you have now become.

Remember, no two things can exist in the same space at the same time. I'll give you another example. If you're vibrating at a frequency of honor and loyalty you're going to be a magnet for honor and loyalty. If you're vibrating at a frequency of infidelity and betrayal, you're going to be a magnet for infidelity and betrayal. The last piece of advice I would like to offer you is that when you are really managing yourself with honor and loyalty and when you really stop cheating on yourself you would never question whether or not you should be with someone who might betray you by cheating on you. If you think about it, being with someone who might do that to you is a form of cheating and betraying yourself. Remember life is an inside job and for better or worse, if you see it, somewhere you're being it. Thank you, Robert, for writing in and sharing your experience with us today, and I wish you a very powerful transformation.

Warmly, Troy

I would like to complete this section by adding, there will be times when someone cheating on you has more to do with them being full-fledged jerks than anything else. However, if you chose to give your heart to a full-fledged jerk, you might want to look in the mirror and responsibly transform what you see. I'm just sayin'.

Responsibly Powerful Bitches & Sexual Predators

There are two distinct types of sexual offenders. Both types are criminals however one admits to being a criminal and designs his attacks around not getting caught. The other type uses manipulation, intimidation, and threats in place of violence to justify his belief that he is not doing anything against the law.

The first type of offender is the one who admits his behavior is criminal and proceeds anyway. This predator hangs out in dark alleys, hides in buildings, breaks into homes and does whatever he needs to do to apprehend his victim. This type of sexual offender is crystal clear that he is a criminal and other than gaining sexual gratification, again, his only hope is that he does not get caught.

The second type of sexual offender is the least threatening of the two at face value but is, in my opinion, the most dangerous of them all. This individual is often a person of great power and authority. He is also usually someone the victim knows, respects, wants to impress, wants to work for and someone she wants to trust. Again, this is an individual who does not believe his sexual behavior is criminal at all. He refuses to manage himself as a sexual predator or criminal because he has done an excellent job rationalizing and justifying his criminal sexual interactions as acts of bartering more than anything else. For most of these type of offenders, their internal dialogue sounds something like, "she's going to give me this, and in exchange, I'm going to give her that." He is often beyond certain that his only fault is the coercing and convincing he has to do and in his mind, that is more taxing than it is a crime. This sexual offender is also more inclined to commit sex crimes in communities where sexual violence is ignored or goes unpunished.

As a female veteran actress, writer, and director I am a member of the #MeToo movement. Me too as in, I too have been sexually assaulted by men in powerful positions, longing to make promises to me in the dark. I can honestly say, I had never felt so disgusted in my life as I did when men in powerful positions attempted to literally, do me. The wrath bestowed upon me for not conceding to their sexual advances followed me for many years. I will never forget the night I was at a Hollywood party, and one of the most powerful, married, studio heads in Hollywood snarled at me in front of an older famous actress. I knew why he was giving me the evil eye. He had been sexually harassing me for years. I never gave into his advances and clearly; he was still pissed off at me because of it. After giving me the evil eye for a few seconds more, he then looked at the older actress and barked, "stay away from Troy, she is dangerous." Instantly obeying him, she gave me the once over and took off with him. I was stunned. I don't know why, but something in me had hoped she would stand up for me instead of walking away from me by his side.

In retrospect, given the older actresses age, of course, I understand why she chose to side with him instead of me. She needed to work, and he was always hiring. However, at the time, I was left with the experience of being sad. Sad that standing up for myself and choosing not to be a Hollywood whore was an expensive choice on so many levels. My sexual harassment and sexual assaults in Tinsel town occurred during a time in my life when I had no idea that being a Responsibly Powerful Bitch was even an option. Not that I dressed like a whore but there were certain reckless bitch behaviors that I participated in, and it is truly by the grace of the universe that harassment and assaults were the extents of my sexual abuse experience in that town.

I often accuse the universe of having a hell of a sense of humor. I believe, there are times the universe will dangle a beautiful Prada purse before us just to test us and see if we have learned our lessons. Case and point, a few years ago, shortly after completing my Master's Degree, I received a phone call from a successful writer/director who was strongly considering me to direct a new film he wrote. I told him I wasn't really in the business anymore and that I was focusing more on my career in the mental Healthcare profession. Still, he insisted that I was most likely the one that he wanted to direct his film. He assured me the pay would be twice the amount earned on my last film, and he asked me if I would simply consider meeting with him before I turned him down. With my grad school tuition in mind and the fact that I could use a few nice new purses, I agreed to at least take a meeting with him.

The writer/director dude thanked me for my willingness to meet, and he told me that his assistant would be calling me within the next 10 minutes to set up a time and a place. His assistant did exactly as he said she would. However, when she gave me his home address, I informed her that I do not meet people in their homes or hotel rooms. I suggested that we meet in a well-known hotel restaurant near his home. She was stunned by request and told me she would have to call me back. He immediately called me back, insulted beyond words. He then demanded that I stop what I was doing and that I check his Internet Movie Data Base (IMDB) page because I obviously had no idea who I was dealing with. At this point had I been living life from my head as a reckless bitch I would have cussed him out from A to Z and hung up on him. However, because I had already begun living my life through my heart's intelligence I quickly moved out of my head and into my heart. Then speaking from my heart, I informed him that my intention was simply to maintain my level of comfort and if he found that to be insulting, I apologize.

Mr. Hot-Shot-Movie-Dude refused to accept my apology and quickly disconnected the call. As the phone line went dead, I had three thoughts; one, I thought about how nice it was to experience such a feeling of calmness on the heels of such a challenging situation. Two; I was very proud of the Responsible Bitch that showed up to powerfully voice and protects my needs. Three; I could not help but to believe that he had ulterior motives. Especially since the movie he wanted me to direct? Yeah, it never happened.

Yes, I concluded that whole thing was one big universal test. I'm pretty sure; the universe simply wanted to see if I was ready to walk my talk. I apparently passed the test with flying colors because on the day after that phone call; I went to the mailbox to find a huge residual check waiting for me from the last film I directed. Guess what I did that following weekend? Yep, I drove to Prada on Rodeo Drive, and I bought myself a new purse!

At this point, I feel compelled to share a few things I have learned over the years when it comes to protecting ourselves from sexual predators, aka reckless dicks! The first thing I want to say about men, all men, is that they are far more visually stimulated than women. Research shows when men see a woman they find desirable the reward center in their brain lights up. This is the same region of the brain that lights up when they see food. Get the point? So the definitive question here is, what defines desirable?

Knowing men the way I think I know men, I would have to say, the more skin shown the more desirable a woman may look. I am by no means suggesting that we not make ourselves desirable but I am suggesting we manage the amount of skin we reveal depending on the situation. I just think there is fundamentally something off about exposing huge amounts of cleavage or butt cheek if you are going into a business meeting. Please do not get it twisted; I love bringing the girls out and showing off my curves if I am going out with my man. Getting your sexy on is also highly recommended if you are single and going out with the hopes of meeting a nice man.

There is a time and place for everything and knowing that time and place could very well be the thing that brings you home safely at the end of your day. Granted, if you left your house butt ass naked, that still does not give anyone the right to violate you in anyway shape or form. I agree. And, truly we should be able to dress however we want when we want. However, the world we live in today does not give a shit about our "shoulds." How do I know this to be the truth? I know this to be the truth because we live in a world where we *should* be able to watch a movie in the movie theater without catching a bullet. Sadly, we live in a world where we *should* be able to drop our kids off at school with absolute certainty that we will be picking them up from school and bringing them home at the end of the day. Sadly, we live in a world where we *should* be able to attend an outdoor concert on a beautiful fall night in Las Vegas without having to run for our lives. I think you get my point. So, yes, we *should* be able to show as much skin as the law permits when we leave our homes, I agree. However, thanks to far too many reckless dicks in this world, our righteous stand for *shoulds* could do more damage to us than good. So, sure, get your sexy on but just be certain you are doing it in a space that is appropriate and safe.

Speaking of spaces now would also be a great time to underscore the importance of meeting places. The bottom line is, if you go into any contained or isolated space with a man, be prepared to have sex with him. If you're not prepared to have sex, then don't go into that space because there will always be a fifty-fifty chance that the person you are in there with will want to engage in some sexual activity with you. And, because the space is contained, you will not have the freedom to come and go as you please. I know this is tough talk but this situation is tough, and it is time for us to stop pretending it will never happen to us. A Responsibly Powerful Bitch would never choose to meet a man in any space that would prevent her from freely walking the fuck out the door if she chose to do so - believe that. She would not care if it was a hotel room or a castle, if she could not leave without having to push through a human or other physical barriers, she would never step over that threshold from the get got.

The last thing I'd like to remind you of is the difference between reacting and responding - it is the difference between coming from your head and coming from your heart. I understand this shift can be very challenging when your safety is at stake. I know it is so easy to just let the head take over. However, remember that when the head takes over, chances are you will soon be operating from your reptilian brain. Whereas if you can drop into your heart's intelligence, your heart's intelligence knows how to protect you better than anyone. The last thing you want to do, when you feel that you're being assaulted on any level, is to lose your bearings or to lose your power. And always keep this in mind, a Responsible Bitch's power moves but is never moved.

Emotion Regulation Technique #5 - Capacitar Anger Management Techniques

Once again, I want to remind you that knowing the triggers, buttons, and techniques I will teach you only work if you are willing to make the conscious effort to make them work. Even then, there will be times that you will not be able to avoid the experience of anger. However, you will have the knowledge and the ability to diminish the duration of your anger and the impact it has on your body. The second emotion regulation techniques I will be teaching you were introduced to me while I spent a semester in grad school studying the healing techniques presented by a global healing organization known as Capacitar®.

"Capacitar's mission is to heal ourselves and heal our world. We teach simple holistic wellness practices that help people tap into the wisdom of their own body, mind, and spirit. This leads to healing, wholeness, and peace in the individual and in the world."

-Capacitar Organization (TM)

What I like about Capacitar's® healing techniques is that they offer healing remedies that nicely compliment the techniques you learned in chapter three from HeartMath™. Capacitar's® healing techniques are also equally effective on their own.

Holding Your Energy Field

The first of the three Capacitar® techniques I want to share with you will help you maintain your energy field while in the space of energy drainers. I refer to such people as energy vampires. Clearly, that needs no explanation. The holding your energy field technique is also great to use when someone is trying to convince you to do something that you do not want to do, and they are attempting to wear you down with various forms of persuasion. Although the instructions are simple, this technique works best seated.

1. While seated, cross your right foot over the left foot.
2. Face your open palms towards each other and allow your fingertips and thumbs to touch each other firmly. This should form a diamond shape between your two hands. Allow your hands to remain in this position as you rest your hands gently on your lap.
3. Relax your shoulders
4. Breathe comfortably (preferably five seconds in, eight seconds out)
5. In this energy-closed system posture, see if you can remain present to your energy as it channels through

your fingers and circulates throughout your body, mind, and spirit

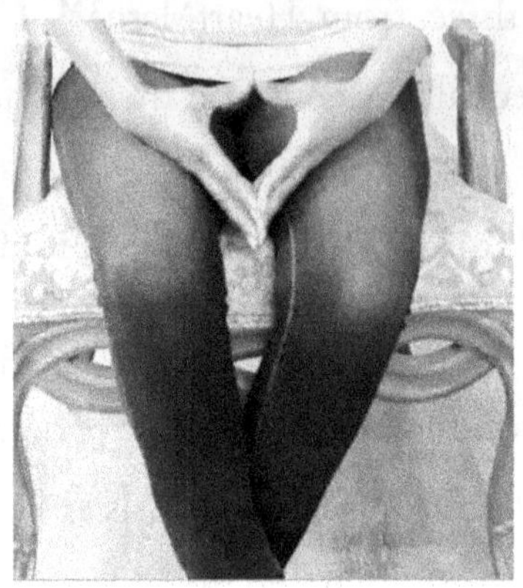

Balancing Emotions with Your Finger Holds

The second Capacitar® influenced emotion regulating technique I want to share with you is another simple process that you can do anywhere, anytime. This technique is all about balancing your emotions by squeezing the finger that correlates with specific emotions. (see list below). This technique works wonders when and if you find yourself in a full-blown reckless bitch mode or close to it. I often urge my angry clients to squeeze the finger that best represents their current emotional state while discussing their issue with me. It makes a huge difference when it comes to interrupting cortisol surges. The reason this technique makes such a difference is that when we are in the midst of a fight or flight reaction, there is often an avalanche of emotions pulsing throughout our bodies. These are the very pulses that we can use as indicators to help us monitor our emotional balance.

The theory here is that energy Channels and Meridians are

located on specific areas of each of our fingers. These Channels and Meridians are correlated with specific emotions and organs. When you hold your finger in the manner depicted in the images below, you ignite the draining process of these emotions while stimulating the flow of energy. Once you take hold of your finger, in a matter of minutes, you will experience an energy pulse or throbbing-like feeling. These pulsing and throbbing sensations are confirmations that the energy is moving and emotional balance is being restored. Shortly after feeling the energy pulse or the throbbing like feeling, there will be a noticeable shift in your emotion as well as your perception of the confronting situation.

Fingers & Correlated Emotions

Thumb Finger – tears, grief, emotional pain

Index Finger – fear & panic

Middle Finger – anger & rage

Ring Finger – anxiety & worry

Pinky Finger – lack of self-esteem

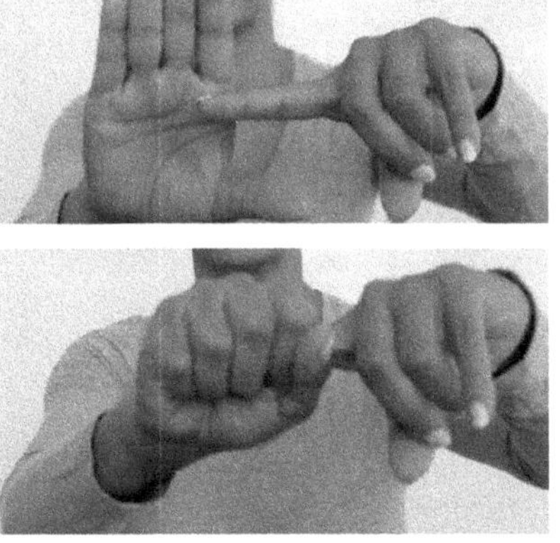

Head Hold

The head hold technique is a great technique to use on a person who is hysterical and/or emotionally out of control. This particular head hold is one you can do on yourself or another. It works great for children and adults. The theory behind this hold is that when the energy of the hands is gently placed on the front part of the brain as well as the base of the skull, it stimulates a quick soothing experience of harmony.

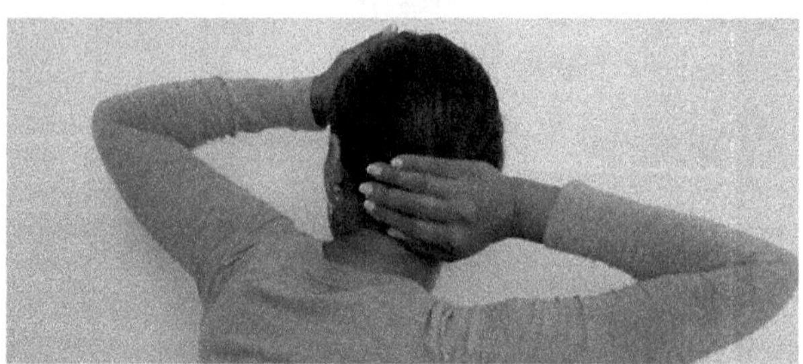

CHAPTER 7
RESPONSIBLY POWERFUL BITCH TRICKS

Awakening the Trickster Hero in You

"The feminine trickster hero aims high, often ignoring the disagreeable nature of uncharted territory. She envisions turning the tables one hundred and eighty degrees, making clear the absolute necessity, the terrible tragedy of excluding the wiles of the feminine in facing uncertainty. If she doesn't guarantee a happy ending, she surely gives us the opportunity to make up the future as we go along." -- Jane Alexander Stewart, Ph.D., University of Alabama

Generally speaking, life can be tricky. When confronted with stressors, threats or challenges, our tricky lives can become slippery slopes and before we know it, we are struggling to crawl out of a deep hole that we somehow managed to fall into face first. Needless to say, attempting to crawl out of deep holes is yet another tricky endeavor.

I once read a quote by musical legend Quincy Jones that said, "when we find ourselves in a deep hole, stop digging." Certainly, that's great advice once and if we find ourselves in any kind of a hole. However, if you haven't figured it out by now, I'm all about prevention as opposed to survival. This is where the archetype of the Trickster comes in. Prior to attending grad school at Pacifica Graduate Institute, I did not know anything about archetypes. As mentioned in chapter six, I knew a lot about stereotypes and what it meant to be a reputation in a community but archetypes, "what's that?" I remember thinking. According to Carl Jung, the modern language of power is expressed through archetypes (Jung, 1990, p.61).

We all fall under the spell of some sort of archetype possession be it a conscious or unconscious choice. I am inviting you to consciously make a point of taking on the Trickster archetype and here's why. In spite of what we were taught to believe, the trickster archetype represents the type of person who stands for liberation, redemption, willingness and the ability to escape from unjust circumstances. She learns the rules of the game extremely well just in case she might need to break them in order to outwit an injustice done to her or someone worthy of her support. The female Trickster has been woman's traditional role in folklores for centuries. Two of my favorite historical and modern day female Tricksters are Rosa Parks and Erin Brockovich.

What makes the Trickster so powerful in her world is her willingness to master and abide by the rules, until she has to make other choices. As a matter of fact, she knows the rules of her world so well that she could break them and make new ones and most people would not even notice until after her intended result has been produced. Their response is then sparked with wonder as they ask, "what happened?" Or "How did she do that?" She's a Trickster, that's how. Now mind you, a Trickster is often confused with the Magician archetype or the Joker archetype. Herein lies the difference: the Jokester's intention is to make people laugh often at the expense of others, and his laughter is often wicked. The Magician's intention is to cause people to believe in a power beyond themselves, leaving them feeling in awe, spooked and intimidated. The Trickster's intention is to, quite frankly, beat the system—systems that were not designed in her best interest or the best interest of those she chooses to support. It is safe to assume, if a person or community is imprisoned, hands down their liberator will be the Trickster archetype.

Tricksters approach life from the perspective of "who does this trick benefit?" Unapologetically a self-advocate, the Trickster's second string of loyalty is bestowed upon those less fortunate people in the world. The Trickster has a soft place in her heart for the underdogs of society because she too has survived the underworld. As a result of her lived experiences, the Trickster is fearless and fierce and a master at defying wit. The Trickster is a priceless member of society and possesses no enemies because she is willing to cooperate with everyone - she truly wants everyone to win but she has no shame in her game when it comes to taking care of herself first. She profoundly understands the consequences for others if she does not make it a point to put her oxygen mask on first.

At this point, I trust you are understanding the persona of the Trickster archetype and how her characteristics serve as the cornerstone for the Responsibly Powerful Bitch. As you may have gathered by now, being responsible can be a tricky endeavor. Point blank, you have to be on top of your shit and of pretty much everyone around you. You have to know your game, your intention and how you want to play it and be played by it. Responsibility comes down to making conscious, informed choices and then daring to re-choose if you don't like the reality your choices are related to. The ability to do so can be tricky and, again, place you on a slippery slope.

What follows in this chapter are several powerful tricks you might want to learn and live by as you strengthen your Responsible Bitch skills. Remember, when you learn the trick, you cannot be tricked and learning the trick is all about mastering the rules, aka knowing the tricks of the trade. In this case, the trade is called Having It All!

How To Manage Your Emotions & Moods with Food

"Let your food be your medicine and your medicine be your food." -

-Hippocrates

Before I dive knee deep into this first bag of tricks, let me preface it by saying, although I do hold a doctorate in clinical psychology, I am not a medical nor am I a licensed nutritionist. What I am is a Responsibly Powerful Bitch who chooses to alter my unwanted moods, organically, by the foods I eat. For the record, there have been times in my life when I considered pharmaceutical medication as a possible solution to mood management. I say that only to say, if pharmaceuticals are or have been your choice for mood regulation, then kudos to you for doing what you believe you needed to do for you. I do not offer the following information as a substitute for pharmaceuticals. Again, I am only sharing my lived experiences with food and the positive impact these foods have made in my life and continue to make when it comes to shaking myself out of a funk.

Many years ago, I stumbled across a headline that read, "There

Is Not A Disease On Planet Earth That The Earth Hasn't a Cure For." The headline resonated with such truth for me, I regret that I did not bother to read the article. However, as a result of that headline, over the years, I kept an eye out for evidence to support both the article and my innate beliefs about our planet and the diseases that plague its occupants. Over the years, I learned how the color and shape of certain fruits and vegetables are good for certain bodily organs that they resemble as indicated in the chart below.

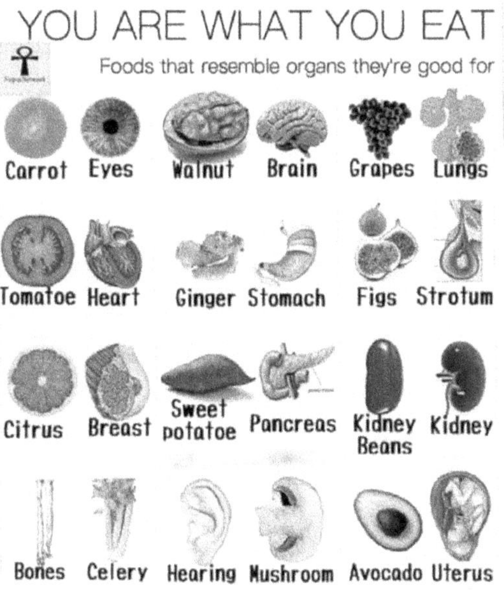

What I did not anticipate discovering during my medicinal food match inquiry is how these easily accessible foods would also be scientifically proven to organically alter and regulate moods in such a quick and powerful way. Research now proves that the medicinal value of food extends beyond physical health – impacting emotions and mental health as well. (http://www.eatthis.com/bad-mood-foods/)

For the sake of convenience and comprehension, I have categorized the most common mood swings most people deal with and then organized the food to correlate with the particular mood swing, according to its medicinal value.

Depression & Anxiety

Almonds
Anchovies
Asparagus
Bananas
Black Beans
Dark Chocolate
Eggs
Green Tea
Granola
Honey
Quinoa
Rice (Brown)
Salmon
Spinach
Green Tea
Yogurt (Greek)

Stress

Avocados
Asparagus
Blue Berries
Buckwheat
Pancakes
Cashews
Chamomille
Tea
Chocolate
Garlic
Grass Fed Beef,
Oatmeal,
Oranges,
Oysters,
Walnuts

The trick to using foods to help keep your reckless bitch at bay is preparation. Your sanity depends on you stocking up on several items from the Depression, Anxiety or Stress list. For example, I always keep almonds in a dish on the coffee table. If I happen to simply come across a story that's bothersome while surfing the web, I pop a few almonds in my mouth to intercept any possible negative biochemical reaction that might occur. In other words, when it comes to managing your mood swings, the Trickster in you must make it her business to stay ahead of the mood swing game. In my commitment to really stay ahead of the game, I have pre-selected the main course, a side dish, a beverage and a dessert that are my "go-to" mood-altering food selections. I know these food combinations work for me and I depend on them when the going gets tough.

My Go-To Mood Shifting Food Combination Choices Are:

Turkey Burger with Sweet Potato Fries

This combination is my absolute go to when I am feeling blue. (I substitute a lettuce wrap for the bun) It might be a placebo effect but who cares, when I eat this meal I swear I can just feel the tryptophan in the turkey going to work on my serotonin levels. I am not sure if it is the vitamin B6 in the sweet potatoes that boost my mood as scientifically proven or if I am in heaven because I love sweet potato fries. Nevertheless, this meal always leaves me feeling much happier than I was before devouring it.

Pineapple & Orange Combination

This is one of my favorite mood altering dessert combinations because the yellow and orange look so pretty side by side. Ironically, research proves that simply looking at the combination of these two fruits releases neurotransmitters responsible for easing depression. When we combine these two fruits, there is molecular compatibility that does wonders for our mood.

Collard Greens & Tomatoes Combination

I was raised on collard greens and I love them. I am not crazy about tomatos, but in this combination they are stewed with the greens, and I love it! The medicinal fact about this combination is the lycopene and vitamin B found in these vegetables and together they do a great job altering my mood.

Coffee with Cinnamon – Great for Anger & Anxiety

Coffee increases dopamine and serotonin, both of which are known as *feel-good* neurotransmitters. Cinnamon clears the mind and makes it easier to process one's thoughts and find clarity in the midst of the chaos.

Chamomile Tea

This tea is powerful due to its ability to increase serotonin and melatonin hormones, both of which have been proven to eliminate stress and anxiety.

How to Be a Skinny Responsibly Powerful Bitch

Let's be real; if you are a female and you have a pulse, you care about how your ass looks in them jeans and the appearance or disappearance of your muffin top over those same jeans. However, with all due respect, I must add a disclaimer for those of you women who really have no concern with being overweight or if you happen to be one of those women who are naturally fit or thin. In that case, what follows is more of a weight maintenance conversation for you as opposed to a weight management conversation for the rest of us.

Before I dive into the Trickster approach to staying skinny or getting skinnier, I want to underscore a few unfortunate facts about the lack of weight management and maintenance. According to research, obesity among American women is at an all-time high (cbsnews.com). And guess what, according to the American Psychological Association, female stress levels are also at an all-time high, stress that in turn is being expressed as anger (apa.org). As I said before, when people know better, most do better. Here is the paradox: we all know how to lose weight, diet and exercise. Yet, how many of you over the age of fifty-five are eating less, working out more and still gaining weight - especially around your abdominal area? Well, what if I told you that your working out is one of the very things that are causing you to gain weight? Shut the front door! I know, right? Who would think such a thing? I'll tell you who, a Trickster committed to being a Responsibly Powerful Bitch about her body and the changes her aging body is going through. You see, when we indulge in strenuous exercise, sure it may be good for certain muscles in our bodies, including the heart, but after forty plus years of dealing with stress, our bodies register almost all strenuous emotions or physical movement as stressful. And, as a biochemical law, when we experience stress, our bodies get busy releasing stress hormones, especially cortisol. When we have large amounts of extra cortisol floating around in our system, our bodies get to work building and storing fat to absorb the excess cortisol in order to protect our organs from absorbing the toxic hormone. As you know, the majority of vital organs are located in the abdominal area. So, that muffin top is really a cortisol sponge, there to soak up the excess hormone before it reaches your organs. In other words, your belly fat is there to protect you from developing diseases that can be fatal. When I learned this, I suddenly became very grateful for my cellulite-ridden abdomen and thrilled that I now knew how to get rid of it.

So, what does a Responsibly Powerful Bitch who embodies the Trickster archetype do with this kind of information? She tricks the system of course! However, the first thing I did was, I thanked my body for doing what she needed to do to keep me safe from cortisol toxicity over the years. I then researched all the physical activities I participated in that were scientifically proven to put stress on my soon-to-be-fit and fabulous body. Sadly, I had to give up all physical activities that were forms of intense aerobic endurance training. So, I gave up my spinning class, my fencing lessons and jogging. In their place I now ride my bike outdoors, I plan to start Tai Chi lessons in place of fencing, I do mild hikes that are, for the most part, long leisurely walks and of course yoga – always yoga. And if you are wondering if the trick worked, I will just proudly say that summer was not only the first time that I wore a bikini in public, but I had the audacity to post the picture on my Instagram. Whoop! Whoop! Whoop!

How To Be Unfuckable With & Loving at The Same Time

Let me preface this story by saying, I am in no way setting a stage for a pity party. I also would like to reiterate the importance of surrounding yourself with people of like mind and loving only those you truly believe to be your worthy opponents. That being said, one day, while looking back at my life, I was like WTF? It dawned on me that I had been hurt and drop kicked to the curb by just about everyone I had ever truly loved - beginning with my parents and yes, even silly Kermit the Frog. This realization really haunted me and I started to question myself on every level because after all, I was the one common denominator in the equation. I started to think: maybe

I was not as committed to making a difference in the lives of others as I believed myself to be over the years. I started to give way to the possibility that I was the fake person my former loved ones accused me of being while metaphorically kicking me in the heart. I even entertained the possibility that I might very well be every bit of the loser in disguise most of them accused me of being. Yes, I went there. I had to go there. I had to figure out whether I was really dealt such a shitty hand in life or if I had created my shitty reality because I was secretly just a straight up shitty person.

I will take a pregnant pause here just to say, this is the part of being a Responsibly Powerful Bitch that gets hard. There is nothing comfortable about examining the validity of negative comments made about you. It's simply an uncomfortable but necessary responsibility – most of the time. Even still, this is the space in which the Trickster longs to be the Jokester archetype who would merely laugh wickedly into the face of reality. It's the space where the Magician archetype would swiftly make it all just disappear, choosing instead to live a life designed by her own illusions. However, I was done with being hurt by people I so-called loved. I wanted to be unfuckable with. I wanted to be a real Trickster, true and through. So, I moved forward with this inquiry, convinced and prepared for the journey to hurt like hell. I promised myself that I would not look away until I saw what I needed to see.

Although I am a huge advocate of just about every form of psychology-based therapy, I knew I had to bring in the big gun for this journey. I knew I had to bring my question to an ayahuasca plant medicine ceremony and so I did. Traveling to Costa Rica, I joined a group of fifteen fabulous people who were also seeking to be emotionally, physically or mentally cured by the medicinal plant ayahuasca. Ayahuasca comes from plants primarily found in the Amazon jungle. Shamans, who remain in a constant state of prayer during the preparation, usually do the cooking of the medicine. The medicine is then served in the form of a tea. Shortly after ingesting the tea, individuals find themselves in a deep, altered state of consciousness where they have access to profound truths about themselves and the world. While journeying on ayahuasca, you are able to bypass the subjective mind and enter into a space that talk therapy would take years if not decades to access. I have to admit, after nearly thirty years of working in the world of transformation and psychology, the personal progress I experienced as a result of ayahuasca is incomparable to anything I have ever done before – the results are absolutely priceless. For the record, I do not do drugs and that includes weed, trees or whatever the cool word is for pot these days – it is just not my thing. Side bar: I do believe weed is also a plant medicine and if it works for you, then I am happy for you.

Prior to embarking upon my ayahuasca journeys, I always make a point of writing down my intention and any questions I wanted to answer to while on the medicine. The interesting thing about ayahuasca plant medicine is that it will always answer you but the answer almost never shows up the way you would expect it to. I have also learned that the manner in which one receives their healing while on the medicine can be emotionally and or physically challenging and if you do not consciously request that your entire journey exists inside of the space of grace and in perfect ways, you might be in for a bumpy ride. Honestly, in spite of my requesting my journey be experienced through grace and in perfect ways, I did not see how that would be possible. After all, I was asking why people I love hurt me. The answer is bound to make one sob uncontrollably and maybe experience the pain all over again. I remember thinking, I have cried so deep, so hard and so often in my life, I just did not feel I had that kind of a cry left in me and if I did, I feared it would be the end of me. And yet, I knew I would be in good hands, I knew I had to trust the medicine.

On this particular night, as the ceremony began, I jumped right into it and asked point blank, "Why is it that the only people who have ever broken my heart were the ones I loved and that I actually gave my heart to?" I then nervously waited for the answer. The best way I can describe the communication process during ceremony is that you hear a voice that has no voice, just information that you instantly comprehend. Growing impatient, I gently asked my question again. Instantly, I then heard, "The people you love hurt you because they are the only ones who could get to you - no one else could get to you." "Ah, so, I'm the fool?" I thought. I paused waiting for more. I needed more because I needed to learn how to be unfuckable with and I was willing to do whatever it took to get there. And then I finally heard, "Troy, the emotion that gets you into situations is the same emotion that will get you out of situations. You always get out through the same door you got in – always remember that." Off my confused silence, I then heard "You heal your heart, the same way they broke your heart. You do it with love. Love got you there, love will get you out." Although my conscious mind could not yet grasp the magnitude of that message, my soul felt it. And in a split second, the young woman across from me startled me for a second as she began crying from the depth of her soul. She continued sobbing and repeating over and over again, "I just love you, that's all." As I listened to her words being released from the deepest crevices of her heart, I recognized and owned every syllable as if they were coming from my mouth instead of hers. I then realized, she was screaming and crying out the words I longed to say to everyone who ever hurt me: "I just love you, that's all."

Although I could still hear and feel the young woman's cries, I fell into a peaceful trance. And every time she screamed, "I just love you, that's all," I imagined myself saying those exact words as I looked into the eyes of each and every person who had ever hurt me in my entire life. Then it all started to make sense, I remembered what I heard from the medicine earlier, "I must use the same emotion to get out of the situation that got me into the situation. Love got me in the situation, only love could get me out." "That's it!" I'm almost sure I whispered out loud and continued to do so. "If I forget the hurt that happened and just get back to the fact that I just love them, that's all, there is no hurt because by returning to the original love, love is all there is.

Now before you accuse me of drinking the Kool-Aid instead of the medicine, hear me out. If Prince had access to and was able to break my heart because I loved him, then I must be able to heal my heart because I loved him. If love is the emotion that got me there, love is the emotion that can get me out of there because anything after my memory of loving him, is not love, it's pain. Again, shifting into reverse, I back up to get away from and delete the hurt and return to the love. When I realized that all the hurt I had suffered over the years was the direct result of me disconnecting from the love I originally had for the person who hurt me, I was flabbergasted. Elated with relief, joy and power, I felt the letter "S" being branded into my chest and I saw my scarlet red cape blowing over my back, in the wind.

While lost in my trance and my newfound realization, I did not notice that the young woman across from me had stopped crying and was now sleeping peacefully. Certain my journey was also over for the night, I rolled onto my stomach and held my pillow gratefully. I finally felt free to love again. Free from the fear of being hurt again. What a life altering night I thought as I sighed, certain that would be my last thought until morning. "Troy?" I heard. "Oh, my…" I said to myself, certain there would now be more. I then heard, "Troy, given what you have learned tonight and because you will soon become an expert at choosing your worthy opponents, chances are very good your experience of others hurting you will be minimal from this point on." A big Kool-Aid smile reshaped my tired face. Then, there was more. "You will come across some very mean people on your life path. It's inevitable." Well, it was a nice smile while it lasted. "And when you come across these mean people, you must find it your heart to authentically tell them the three words most mean people rarely hear. You must say, "I love you." They need to hear those words to heal." In no way aligned with wishing mean people love, I promised to do so anyway only because history had proven that the information obtained during my journeys never leads me astray. I also knew my heart understood the medicine's intention and in time my heart would help my head to understand as well.

What I did not know is that my heart teaching my head the lesson would happen so darn soon. Shortly after my "how to be unfuckable with" journey, I allowed a guy who had hurt me terribly in my past to come back into my life. Truth be told, he caught me at a very weak time in my life – a time when everything felt like an uphill battle. He told he how much he missed me. He told me that I would forever be the love of his life and that with every sunrise and sunset he saw my face and heard my laughter. Yeah, I believed his every word and well, okay, you can put the "L" on my forehead for a moment. And yes, with all of my training and development, I fell prey to the wolf dressed in sheep's clothing. To my credit, I also still loved him and I had secretly hoped that one day he would sober up, get his act together and really show up as my worthy opponent. I won't bore you with the details but I will say, a leopard never changes his spots. Within one month's time, he had lured me in with deceptive behavior and then drop kicked my heart to the curb twice as hard as he had the first time.

Deception being my trigger, the reckless bitch in me was immediately activated. I felt the cortisol surging through my body as my heart rate drastically increased. I wanted to react venomously and immediately. I wanted to hurt him the way he had just hurt me. Fortunately, as all the ugly was happening, I managed to drop from my head into my heart. I never remembered the distance being so damn far – but I did it. I began doing my Heart Focus breathing while doing the Capacitar middle finger hold to reduce the rage and anger progressively rising up in my body.

My reckless bitch desires to destroy kept trying to pull me away from my heart focus breathing and as much as I wanted to give in, I couldn't. My heart reminded me that I deserved so much more than being hijacked by my primitive brain. My head argued that I should fight his ass tooth and nail like I used to do when he tried to hurt me. Yet, I knew my heart was right. I knew I deserved more than saturating my body with stress hormones and eventually behaving like a cave woman. I also knew this was a prime opportunity for me to walk my talk. And, so I did. I continued to focus on my heart's nostrils as if my life depended on it - five seconds in and eight seconds out. After a few more seconds of Heart Focus breathing, my reckless bitch desire completely subsided. There was no anger or urge to fight to be found in me – none at all. That realization moved me to tears because for the first time, I experienced the me that I always wanted to be.

Today, I remain profoundly grateful for that experience because in many ways, it served as an on-the-court opportunity for many things to come full circle for me. Some times in life we don't really know how far we have come until we find ourselves back where we began – even if only for a short while. Remembering the promise

I made to the medicine, after politely addressing some of the very mean things that person said to me in his email, I then simply replied, "I just love you, that's all." Anything after that would only be wasted attention directed at an unworthy opponent.

I must say, out of all the tricks in the book, the trick to being unfuckable with is one certainly worth mastering. To recap, the trick simply entails taking the following two steps: The minute you are hurt and you shift into reverse, away from the hurt and hang out in the original space of, "I just love you, that's all," you are unfuckable with. The second you are able to send love where there is no love, you are unfuckable with. Why? Because when others choose to manage conflict from their heads, hijacked by primitive behavior, we Responsibly Powerful Bitches manage our affairs from a higher intelligence, our heart's intelligence, a space negativity simply cannot reach. Granted, we won't become masters at being unfuckable with overnight, but the heart is a muscle and like any muscle, the more you exercise it, the more you will be able to use it. To answer my original question, I now know I was not born with a shitty hand and I don't have shitty experiences because I am a shitty person. The bold face truth is: life can be challenging and shit happens. The question is, when shit happens, who are you going to be about it? Well, like me, there will be times you might relapse and fall prey to the wolves of life dressed in sheep's clothing – it might happen, you might go there. The good news is this: as a Responsibly Powerful Bitch, with Trickster skills, for sure you won't stay there.

As much as I would like to end this chapter here, this story would not be complete in the telling if I did not circle back around to discuss the young woman who served as my surrogate crier at the beginning of my plant medicine ayahuasca journey. The next morning, the entire group gathered in a circle to debrief about the night before. The young woman, the one who cried out loud over and over again, "I just love you, that's all," raised her hand to share. Then she shyly said, "I came to do plant medicine because I have been suicidal. I have been numb to life for the last two years and ayahuasca was my last hope. I asked the medicine to 'help me feel again, help me cry again, help me love again.' I honestly cannot remember the last time I even shed a tear. During my journey last night, I cried in a way I never imagined possible and it felt so good." I don't think there was a dry eye in the room as she then said, "This may sound weird but I felt safe to really let it out because I felt like someone was crying with me. I mean, I couldn't hear them but I felt them and felt as if they felt me and I dunno, I just felt like we cried together." Without hesitation, I raised my hand as I said, "That was me." Connecting eye-to-eye, we shared a knowingness that I will remember for the rest of my life as we then simultaneously said, "Thank you." I then silently thanked the plant medicine ayahuasca for curing both of us, through grace and in perfect ways. A man in the group then turned toward the woman and asked, "If it's not too personal, can you share who you were talking to when you were saying, 'I just love you, that's all'?" He then added, "You were saying it with a force and magnitude I have never ever heard before, it was beautiful." Smiling softly but proudly she responded, "I was saying it to life."

CONCLUSION

After completing the last chapter of this book, I took some time away from it to reflect on the content, my experience of writing it, and that which stood out the most for me during the process. I found it strange that out of everything I wrote, I was most bothered by the fact that two of the most powerful men in Hollywood referred to me as *dangerous*. Before writing this book, I was not consciously aware of what I will refer to only as a synchronicity since I do not believe in coincidence. That being said, once I became aware of this synchronicity of accusations, I was truly bothered. I started to wonder if there was any truth to these accusations. After all, because they are both powerful, rich, men in Hollywood, surely, they know more than me. "Damn!" I remember thinking as I stopped myself from falling down that self-deprecating rabbit hole. A hole padded with the bullshit opinions others have about me, the very opinions that I so easily once embraced and believed. Just like when Harvey Weinstein gave me the kiss of death after losing the bidding war on my directorial film debut. Not only did I believe him to be right about thunder never striking twice for me, I subconsciously set out to make him right.

As I pondered the possibility of me truly being dangerous a bit further, I found myself uncomfortable and wanting to bypass that inquiry and close that chapter for good. But, I learned long ago that issues are a lot like yoga poses. When you lean into the discomfort of an issue, you deepen your connection with spirit and level of awareness about that issue. "Shit!" I thought, and reminded myself that the road to enlightenment is rarely light, but the journey is worth every bit of the illumination. Besides, I should have known the universe would not permit me to write a book such as this without putting my ass on the line – several times. So, doing what I have learned to do with discomfort, the Responsibly Powerful Bitch in me turned towards it and looked it square in the eye. What I immediately saw was that the first accusation of my being dangerous was due to me taking the blame for my friend's reckless bitch behavior when she sent the fire department to her boyfriend's house because she suspected he was cheating on her. Although I did not commit the crime, I lied and I said I did to cover my reckless bitch friend's ass. Taking on accountability for her reckless bitch behavior, by default, made me a reckless bitch too. As cliché' as it sounds, the fact of the matter remains, if you lie down with dogs you wake up with fleas. I concluded, the first accusation of being dangerous was hands down due to my reckless bitch behavior. The reckless bitch behavior that is indeed dangerous enough for us to drive our lives into a ditch.

My second accusation of being dangerous was a direct result of my turning down the sexual advances of a married man who owned the studio that purchased one of my films. My observation led me to conclude that this Hollywood mogul was accusing me of being dangerous because I refused to give in to his endless acts of sexual assault and harassment. Although I did meet with him on several occasions hoping our meetings would eventually become about future business opportunities, I always insisted we meet in public places. I remember one time he actually scolded me for showing up in conservative business attire. He was hoping to see more skin - a lot more. In retrospect, I can see how my Responsibly Powerful Bitch behavior was dangerous regarding intercepting and detonating all of his sexual intentions with me. The Responsibly Powerful Bitch behavior that is indeed capable of taking our lives to new heights.

I wanted to share this observation with you because I believe this experience captures the essence of this book. As women, we cannot always avoid the hormonal, biochemical, cultural or external factors that may inspire and contribute to the anger we have come to know and be known for. However, we can check ourselves before we wreck ourselves. And, we can do this by being responsible for all of our truth, for all that we are, and all that we are not. By doing so, in a cool way, the jig is up. We don't have to show up perfect anymore. We just have to show up responsible. Inside of that context of responsible, we can count on ourselves to be consistently present to the results we want to create. Inside of that context of responsible, we can also hold others responsible for the bullshit they drop or try to create in our space. #NoMore. We don't have to be afraid of our reckless bitch inspired weaknesses anymore. This also means that we don't have to be afraid of our Responsible Bitch inspired power anymore. Surely by now, you know that both bitches live on the same hand, just different sides. And, when we know better, we do better. So, now you know. So, now you decide. Are you going to live on the side of your hand that gives high-five slaps or backhand smacks? That answer depends solely on what you want for your life.

If I had to vote, I vote for your greatness. I vote for your daily experience of giving high-five slaps. I vote for you being as badass in the bedroom as you are in the boardroom and never again having to apologize for having it all and being it all.

I vote for you being powerfully responsible for everything in your life that works and does not work. Because you know, when it comes to your life, it all begins and ends with you, not them. Blaming them is what the reckless bitch does. Claiming who you are is what the Responsibly Powerful Bitch does. Blaming is for renters of life. Claiming is for owners of life. If not now, then when?

I told you I had four specific commitments that I wanted to fulfill by the end of this book.

1) To address the reasons why we, as women, do not chill out when we know darn well we are seconds away from irreversible damage or danger.

2) To demonstrate exactly how formerly reckless bitches can have the lives they want by upgrading their bitch status from reckless bitch to Responsibly Powerful Bitch.

3) To help you understand the origin of your anger triggers and buttons and identify them before they emotionally and blindly take you hostage.

4) To teach you how to access your anger as a powerful source for creating a life you absolutely love.

I would like to believe that I have fulfilled on my intentions. I am choosing to believe that now that you know what there is to know about being a bitch, you are committed to being the baddest bitch you know. I dare you to be dangerous in the best possible ways. I double dare you to be one hundred percent unfuckable with. I triple dare you to do everything in your power to make sure everyone who knows you, knows you to be a Responsibly Powerful Bitch – more importantly, being a Responsibly Powerful Bitch is how you know yourself.

References

Childre, D., Martin, H., & Beech, D. (1999). *The Heartmath Solution*. New York: Harper Collins.

Jack, R. (2014). All human behaviour can be reduced to 'four basic emotions'. Retrieved from www.bbc.com/news/uk-scotland-glasgow-west-26019586

Jung, C. G. (1990). *The Archetypes and the Collective Unconscious* (10 ed.). New York, New York: Princeton University Press.

Lennox, M. (2017, September 19, 2017). Perchance To Dream. *Facebook*. Retrieved from www.facebook.com/permalink.php

Muchinsky, P. M., & Culbertson, S. S. (2016). *Psychology Applied to Work* (11th ed.). Summerfield, N.C.: Hypergraphic Press, Inc.

Rounds, R. (2015). The Female Anger Epidemic. Retrieved from www.dailymail.com.uk/femail/article

Siegal, B. S. (1998). Love, Medicine and Miracles: Lessons Learned about Self-Healing from a Surgeon's Experience with Exceptional Patients. : HarperPerennial.

Stress by gender. (2017). Retrieved from www.apa.org/news/press/releases/stress

U.S. women hit milestone for obesity. (June 7, 2016). Retrieved from www.cbsnews.com

About The Author

Troy Byer is the CEO and founder of Mindology Fit Living; a comprehensive brand dedicated to organic healing and holistic lifestyle solutions. She holds a B.A. in clinical psychology, a master's degree in eco, liberation, and community psychology, and a doctorate in clinical psychology.

Dr. Troy has coached and led workshops for thousands of people worldwide, including working as a transformational seminar leader on behalf of one of the world's largest organizations, focusing on personal and professional growth and development. Dr. Troy has worked with convicted women assigned to her anger management program and continues to build life-altering online and in person communities and workshops.

Please be sure to join Dr. Troy's Circle of friends and become a member of our powerful and supportive Responsibly Powerful Bitch community

https://www.drtroybyer.com/checkyourselfbeforeyouwreckyourself

www.ingramcontent.com/pod-product-compliance
Lightning Source LLC
Chambersburg PA
CBHW072046090426
42733CB00032B/2272

* 9 7 8 0 9 8 0 1 7 6 3 9 1 *